T0378864

# THE
# COMPTON COWBOYS

### AND THE FIGHT TO SAVE
### THEIR HORSE RANCH

# THE COMPTON COWBOYS

## AND THE FIGHT TO SAVE THEIR HORSE RANCH

### WALTER THOMPSON-HERNÁNDEZ

**HARPER**

*An Imprint of HarperCollinsPublishers*

for my mama

# CONTENTS

# THE PARADE

**THE HORSES ON THE RANCH** sensed that one of the largest storms of the year was on the horizon and heading directly toward the farms. On any other weekend, rain wouldn't have been a problem, particularly with the five-year California drought, but on the weekend of the sixty-fifth annual Compton Christmas parade, rain couldn't have come at a more inconvenient time.

Several of the horses at the farms began feeling restless hours before the first gray clouds started to form over the city. They neighed loudly and flapped their long, coarse-haired tails, prompting a cacophony of sounds from other horses in nearby ranches throughout the farms. When the clouds finally did appear, they moved in slowly, deliberately—almost like they were aware of the potential they had to alter thousands of families' weekend plans. The rain started as a light, soft drizzle, growing into a heavy downpour within an hour. Local rain canals, deteriorating from years of neglect, got hit the hardest. They immediately overflowed with trash and local waste as the rushing current headed south toward the Los Angeles River in the direction of the Pacific Ocean.

After listening to a Spanish-radio weather announcement earlier that day, Mr. Sanchez made sure to pack his large blue tarp onto his pickup truck after loading it with fresh meat, tortillas, and an assortment of vegetables that he bought from the market. He always had the fewest clients whenever it rained, and not having a protective covering over his stall drastically affected business.

But when the water began to pour through the tarp and onto the tables and chairs, he knew it was time to pack up his one-man taco stand and head home for the night. "That's it for tonight, amigo," he said to Jerome Jordan, a sixty-five-year-old black man who had worked for him for the past two years directing cars into a nearby abandoned lot in exchange for a few dollars and a plate of *al pastor* tacos at the end of each night. Like others his age, Jerome had lived through both the 1965 Watts Riots and the 1992 Los Angeles Riots and had seen his city go through dramatic changes.

On the ranch, the rain continued to fall on the weary

aluminum tin roofs that protected the horses from the elements. Puddles of cold, muddy water collected in each stall, creating the perfect conditions for the spread of thrush, a bacterium known to thrive in dark, moist conditions and infect horse hooves. The sound of the hard pounding rain had made many of the horses uneasy. In a matter of months, if money wasn't found to keep the ranch running, the horses would be gone. It was something that Randy Hook, the cowboys' leader, was thinking about on a daily basis.

Helio, one of the largest black Thoroughbreds on the ranch, neighed the loudest and moved erratically in his stall. His size often intimidated the other horses and kept every other horse on guard. Chocolate, a dark brownish old pony, rolled around in the mud, making his coat two shades darker with every turn. Sonny, one of the other quarter horses, aggressively chewed on the metal gate that separated him from Fury. On the opposite side of the ranch, Red Dog, an Australian cattle breed dog, scurried into the barn for protection at the first sight of water and spent the rest of the night curled up next to a bale of hay.

Byron Hook began feeling antsy as he tossed and turned inside his brown-carpeted bedroom. The rain had stopped in the middle of the night, and by morning the sun had finally crept out. He was a big guy for his height, five feet ten inches tall and weighing close to 240 pounds. His brown wooden single bed creaked loudly every time he turned his body in a different direction. The only thing louder was the sound of the Gutierrez family's crowing rooster next door, which had become like an alarm clock for him.

Usually the first one awake on the ranch, Byron was also the earliest to bed after watching the same cowboy westerns that he used to watch with his parents as a child in nearby Harbor City. As one of the last remaining original gangsters on the block, he had lived to see the Richland Farms go through many transformations, and, like the oak and sycamore trees that proudly lined both sides of the streets, he, too, had seen more than he had ever needed to see.

Back in the late 1980s, when the homes on the farms were mostly owned by African-Americans, Byron was known around the neighborhood for his flashy customized lowrider motorcycle. It had a curved banana seat and tall silver-chromed handlebars. The body was painted blue. At one point he attached a homemade speaker system to the back of his bike and played the same CDs that he downloaded and sold for a profit at local swap meets and at lowrider car shows. In those days, five dollars could get you an entire album, ten dollars could get you three, and twenty dollars could get you five. It was how he made his money and friends in the neighborhood. If his nephews, Randy and Carlton Hook, were lucky, he would let them stand on his back pegs and hang on to his shoulders while he rode up and down Caldwell Street.

At fifty-six, however, Byron's health had suffered due to several operations, and his memory was starting to fade. In addition to his failing health, streaming music services like Spotify had put a substantial dent in his music business. With almost no other way to make money, he began to panhandle around the neighborhood, sometimes coming home with a few dollars in his pockets, sometimes with nothing. He was struggling to get by.

On this particular morning, he was waiting for his nephews to arrive before the parade. As often, they arrived late. "What up, Byron?" his nephew Carlton said, abruptly opening the screen door. Carlton was wearing a pair of black sweats, sandals with white socks, and a snug-fitting white tank top.

Carlton sat down on the porch steps, protected from the sun by the overhead roof. His braids hung completely free, just out of the view of his glasses, but low enough to graze the *C* and *H* tattoos on his wiry shoulders. His friend Keenan Abercrombia had inked the tattoo on him in his backyard a few years ago.

"You-you . . . almost hit me with the door, man!" Byron said with a deep stammer. At this point in his life, his speech, much like his body, had diminished and was worsening by the day.

"What you talking about?" Carlton quickly responded. "You trippin'." Carlton's voice rarely ever rose beyond a low murmur. Carlton was quiet and more reserved than his twin brother, Randy, and he preferred the sound of others to his own voice.

"Never . . . never mind it," Bryon said. "You read—ready for the parade?"

"You kiddin'?" Carlton said. "I've been waiting for this day all year, man."

When the city of Compton was incorporated in 1888 by founder Griffith D. Compton, his intention was to create a community where people could farm and cultivate crops. Thirty pioneering families quickly established a tight-knit community founded on agricultural traditions carried over from the Midwest and the South.

What began as a small, rural town emerged as ample residential lots that gave families from all over California the chance to raise a family, care for crops, and tend to livestock. The Richland Farms became a ten-acre community in the heart of Compton, founded blocks away from what would later become the Compton Courthouse and Compton High School. The farms became a community within a community that allowed families to live a semblance of the lives they once lived before.

As one of the only remaining agricultural areas in Los Angeles, the farms always welcomed rainfall. While most people in the city drove in a hurried frenzy and complained about the rain, residents of the farms celebrated its arrival with joy. Nearly every resident who lived in the community came from rural backgrounds in the South and throughout Mexico. Families like Carlton and Randy Hook's, one of the last black cowboy families on the farms, had migrated west from Arkansas during the mid-twentieth century as part of a wave that included thousands of other African-Americans. It was called the Great Migration, a mass exodus of black families who settled in cities throughout the Northern states and in West Coast cities like Seattle, San Francisco, Oakland, and Los Angeles.

In Los Angeles, black families from the South arrived with the hope of working in newly established war-era industries and industrial plants. Many of them were drawn to communities like Central Avenue, a mile-long strip that ran north to south known as the "eastside" of South Los Angeles—one of the only communities in Los Angeles where black families were free from the racially restrictive laws that made it illegal for black families to own property. Until the mid-1950s Compton was still predominantly white and unaffordable for most African-Americans. It was where George H. W. Bush, the nation's forty-first president, lived for six months in 1949 with his wife and his son, future president George W. Bush, when he worked at a nearby security engineering company.

The eventual exodus of white families and the simultaneous closing of factories and plants in the area reduced property prices, slowly bringing more black families to the hub city. Compton's black population rose from 5 percent in 1940 to 40 percent by 1960 and continued to grow as nearby events like the 1965 Watts Riots, which began after local police pulled over an African-American motorist for reckless driving, led to one of the largest uprisings in Los Angeles's history and over forty million dollars in property damage. They simultaneously made middle-class black families move to Compton and white families leave it.

Families like the Hooks eventually chose to live in the farms after living in nearby Harbor City because it reminded them of the lives that their families had left behind in the South. There were trees, animals, and, most of all, the space to roam and be free. Mexican families like the Gutierrezes, the Hooks' next-door neighbors, were also the products of migration. When the Mexican peso fell and trade agreements like the North American Free Trade Agreement radically altered the price of crops in the 1990s, the effects were felt instantly, destroying families like the Gutierrezes' way of life in the process. They, too, were lured by the promise of work, leaving their rural villages in Jalisco, Mexico, to seek a better life, as generations of African-Americans had done decades before them.

That morning, every rain cloud that appeared in the sky the night before was replaced by puffy, cotton-like cumulus clouds. The local forecasters had failed once again. The rain—which they said would last all weekend—lasted only one night, and the parade would continue as planned. As the sun continued to emerge, drops of water dripped from the tin roof stables and into each horse stall, creating a mushy blend of soiled dirt with fresh horse droppings. Because resources had been scarce on the ranch in recent years, fixing the holes in each stall was less important than feeding the animals and paying ranch employees.

It was the biggest day of the year on the farms, and the entire city had woken up beaming with anticipation. The horses were calm now that the storm had passed. Some looked out in the direction of the courthouse, while others peered toward Caldwell Street, sending out the occasional baritone neigh and whimsical tail flip. Red Dog was nowhere to be found, probably hiding in someone else's yard or away on one of the three-day vacations from the ranch he sometimes wandered off on. Only the roosters continued to crow on schedule.

The Compton, Dominguez, and Centennial High School marching bands and step teams had been practicing for weeks for the lead-up to the parade. In between practicing for their Friday night football games, each school had created new routines that would be revealed at the parade.

Centennial was the heavy favorite over the other two, but this year, under the direction of new leadership, Compton

High's band and step teams felt confident about their chances to win the marching band competition as the day approached. Members of each band and team washed and ironed their uniforms the same way the night before the big parade—eagerly waiting to show the city what they had secretly been working on.

For the Compton Cowboys and other horseback riders, the parade had as much to do with pride as it did the need to address safety concerns for horseback riders in the city. The parade was one of the only times of the year when horseback riders could ride safely on the streets without the threat of being hit by traffic, and in recent years, horse and rider deaths had spiked despite pleas by community groups to create more horse lanes near the farms. Speed limits were hardly enforced, and loud car music often spooked horses, causing fatal accidents on some of Compton's busiest streets. The horses were in constant danger.

Riding in the parade would be a way to introduce the Compton Cowboys to the city for the first time since they last rode in the parade over fifteen years ago. Whether or not the other guys knew it, this was a day that Randy had been thinking about for months—he knew how important it was to the future of the group and his aunt's legacy.

This year felt a bit different for the cowboys. They had a lot to prove: it was their first time riding under the CC moniker, and it would be their chance to show friends and family that they could succeed without the supervision of the elders who taught them how to ride when they were children.

More importantly, they wanted to prove to Mayisha that they could do it on their own, particularly because of the disagreements they had had with her about their image. She did not always approve of the way they dressed or rode their horses. Riding horses with house shoes or slippers on was not the way she had taught them to ride. At the same time, it could be one of the cowboys' last parades: their ranch was in danger of closing as their resources dwindled every day. It was something that everyone was aware of.

Horse riding in Compton had become less common, and the sight of riders in the streets was less frequent each year. In the past, as many as five different riding groups rode through the parade, but these days, the only two remaining groups were the Compton Cowboys and Los Rancheros de Compton, a Mexican riding group that usually walked away with the award for best equestrian team each year.

Grooming the horses took up most of the cowboys' time. It's why Keenan, Charles Harris, and Anthony Harris had spent most of the day before the parade washing and brushing their horses in anticipation.

When they arrived to check up on their horses the following morning, an hour after Byron and Carlton met up, the ranch was nearly empty. Only Rashid, Mayisha's eldest son, was around. His dreadlocks were covered by a white bandana as he looked over the gate that connected his home to the rest of the ranch. Since moving back over a year ago, he had kept out of the way of the cowboys, showing his face only when he needed to warm up his breakfast at his uncle Louie's house next door.

Charles's body moved at a slower pace than anyone else's that morning. It had been only a couple of hours since he had gotten off from working the overnight shift at Walmart, and his body was running on adrenaline and cold day-old coffee that he had grabbed on his way out from the employee break room some hours earlier.

"I have to go ride some horses," Charles told his manager earlier that morning as he hurried out, patting the outside of his pants' pockets, looking for his car keys. "Horses?" his manager asked with a surprised look on his face, hardly believing him. "Yeah, horses!" Charles said with a smirk before running out of the room.

Keenan was the only one in the group who hadn't driven to the ranch that morning. Since his license got suspended earlier that year, Uber had become his transportation of choice when his wife didn't have time to drive him. The young expecting couple shared a two-bedroom apartment in Inglewood just big enough for them and her five-year-old daughter and within sight of the construction of the nearby professional football stadium that was threatening to raise their rent.

The past few weeks had been particularly challenging for

the twenty-seven-year-old. It had been almost a month since he was laid off as a sous-chef in a Louisiana-style restaurant near downtown Los Angeles, and every Uber ride to the ranch put a dent in his dwindling bank account.

"Why you always got the dirtiest horse on the ranch?" Charles asked Carlton, who joined the rest of the guys, still wearing the same clothes from his night shift.

"Man, shut up," Carlton replied. "Why you always on my head?"

"I'm just asking," Charles said with a full grin on his face.

Anthony and Keenan laughed loud enough for the next-door neighbor's dogs to start barking. Both friends immediately started an argument between Carlton and Charles, like they had done for the past twenty years. Talking trash to each other was a popular pastime on the ranch. It made time go quicker and brought everyone together.

"You gonna let him talk to you that way?" Anthony asked while continuing to laugh hysterically and grabbing his stomach. "Maaaaaaan . . . I wouldn't!"

Carlton, Randy's quieter, younger twin, was usually the butt of everyone's jokes and an easy target for Charles, who prided himself on being one of the biggest jokesters on the ranch. There wasn't a day that passed when he didn't find an excuse to make fun of someone. He made fun of everything. If it walked, he made fun of it. Nothing got past his observant eyes.

At the same time, Charles was also one of the most sensitive cowboys in the group, whose jokes often masked the insecurities that he felt about himself; finding pleasure in making fun of others deflected from his own shortcomings.

Carlton grabbed Helio, a large black Thoroughbred with long, bushy winter hair, from the stall, walked him to the gate, and tied him up before beginning to brush him. His horse had rolled around in the mud all night and was three shades darker than when he last saw him. After a few more brushstrokes, he threw his brush on the ground and walked back to his house without finishing the only duty he had that morning. Carlton had been friends with Charles since they were children and had grown accustomed to his jokes, but it didn't stop him from being annoyed.

"Man, forget this," he said as he left his horse on the gate and slowly walked away, his sweats hanging far below his waist.

"See?" Charles said while looking at Anthony and Keenan. His smile grew wider with every step that Carlton took away from the group. "He's soft, man. He softer than a baby's booty!"

An hour passed, and the three continued to tend to their horses. It was a practice that they had learned as children and now had perfected as adults. Being near the stables brought them a sense of peace that they had first felt as riders in the Compton Jr. Posse, Mayisha's youth riding organization that had brought them all together as children over twenty years ago. They had learned to clean stalls and groom horses before being able to ride. But grooming the horses' coats wasn't only a way to care for the horses; it was also a way to care for themselves. The ranch became a place where they went to ride horses and stay safe from the dangers that lurked outside on the streets. It was where they went when they ran away from home, and it was where they found peace.

Time had passed, however, and with Mayisha's retirement party quickly approaching and the future of the ranch in jeopardy, their safety, and their way of life, were up in the air.

Anthony noticed Fury's limp when he first arrived at the ranch that morning. Fury was Randy's horse, but Anthony knew his personality better than anyone else on the ranch. After all, he spent the most time with the horses and was the oldest of the cowboys. During the weekdays, Anthony's workday began at five a.m. and lasted well into the early afternoon. It was his job to keep up with all twelve of the horses, to feed and care for them. It had been almost six months since the onset of Fury's phantom limp, which Anthony suspected to be clubfoot, a condition that involved asymmetrical horse hooves.

But Anthony believed the way Fury's horseshoe had been fitted had made his clubfoot even worse. Everyone knew the farrier liked to cut corners when nobody was there to supervise him, and more so, everyone suspected it had to do with race: Did horse ranches run by white families receive the same treatment? Every time Fury stepped on the ground and applied pressure, it created a deep agitation, forcing a limp. If more resources had been available on the ranch, like in the old days with Mayisha, then Fury would have seen a specialist. But with limited funds, all he could do was apply more medication balm to dull the pain.

Back in front of the ranch, on Caldwell Street, there was still no sign of the rest of the cowboys. Only the sounds of Mexican *banda* music played off in the distance while commercial planes and helicopters flew in and out of Compton's local airport.

After the trio finished grooming their horses, they each left to go run different errands. Anthony had to drop off his granddaughter at her aunt's home, Charles drove to the Grape Street housing projects to see his family, and Keenan had to head back home to pick up some riding gear. Kenneth, another one of the cowboys, whose home bordered the ranch's back wall, was nowhere to be found.

Getting each of the ten cowboys to ride together was one of the biggest challenges for the group these days. The cowboy lifestyle that they were living—big street rides, ranch work, and rodeo competitions—were sometimes at odds with the realities of day-to-day life. Only Tre, one of the youngest cowboys and a rodeo champion, and Charles continued to train and compete in their respective events, bareback riding and show jumping. Keiara, the only woman in the group, was still recovering after a back injury that continued to keep her out of barrel racing. The rest of the gang wrestled with the challenge of putting food on the table for themselves and their families, and with growing families and more mouths to feed, they weren't able to go to the ranch and ride regularly.

In the meantime, Randy Hook drove south on Wilmington Boulevard toward the ranch in his dark blue Chevy Malibu. His jet-black tinted car windows rattled with the sounds of heavy bass rap music. Since he had taken over as the Compton Cowboys' leader and begun to take more responsibility with the ranch in anticipation of Mayisha's retirement, his anxiety and stress had drastically increased. The only way to remedy the pressure was to ride his horse alone around the farms at night and take long drives through the city. Driving alone allowed him to sit with his thoughts, away from the reach of those who often relied on him for answers that he didn't always have. He could momentarily escape the pressures of being a father, a brother, and the leader of the last black cowboys in Compton.

As he waited for the light to turn green at the intersection of Alondra and Wilmington, a group of five black teenagers gathered at the cross light. They were no older than fifteen and showed signs of the life he and his friends had once lived. They wore red shoes and jackets and held bags of potato chips and sodas in their hands, the same way he used to. They reminded him of the Akrite party crew that he and the cowboys had created as teenagers as a way to stay together after they left the Compton Jr. Posse, which is what got them riding horses in the first place. The crew threw weekend parties and were known around Compton as one of the best party organizers. Like the Akrites, the group of teenagers stood in formation, creating a 360-degree circle of vision around them for protection. They hung on to each other because they were all they had. Randy thought about his party crew days while looking at the group of teenagers; he and his brother's eighteenth birthday party had left two of their friends dead and forced them to disband and abandon the scene altogether.

In a matter of moments, Randy's nostalgia immediately wore off as some of the people in the group turned to face his direction. In seconds they transformed from friendly, nostalgic reminders into potential threats. They saw only a potential enemy in a dark blue car with tinted windows, not someone who had once stood on the same corner with the same intentions—someone with the same wild spirit. Though Randy was still on neutral territory, he kept a sharp eye on the group. The farms belonged to the Farm Dog Crips, who comprised his friends and family, while the area west of Wilmington Boulevard belonged to their enemies, the Nutty Blocc Crips gang. The group continued to stare at his car, anticipating action.

When the light turned green, Randy quickly tapped his foot on the ignition pedal and sped away, past the 7-Eleven and the Louisiana Fried Chicken, and within seconds the group became small figures in his rearview mirror, like the memories of his youth.

It had been only a few weeks since Randy had started living out of the trunk of his car. His backseats were full of clothes, shoes, and anything else he could find room for. Each of his most prized cowboy hats were gently stacked on top of boxes, leaving only a slight crevice in between two large boxes in the backseat to see out of his rearview mirror.

The apartment that he and his girlfriend had been renting in the San Fernando Valley had gotten too expensive, and with a newborn baby, finding the means to afford the rent was a financial strain on the high school sweethearts. So the young family moved back to the farms, back to the community where they had first met more than fifteen years ago, back to the community they had once left to find peace of mind.

On top of that, Randy had left his job and now hoped to generate an income directing the ranch and its organization when his aunt Mayisha officially retired.

He had big dreams. Living out of his car, however, wasn't

what the twenty-eight-year-old with a college and graduate degree had imagined he would be doing, but it was the only choice he had. His father's house was full, and the middle home on the ranch was better suited for his baby boy, Lux, and the baby's mother, Marriah. Isolating himself helped Randy deal with his anxiety, and spending nights alone was at times the only cure for the insomnia that he had experienced since he was a child.

He made a left at the intersection of Caldwell and Wilmington, at the gas station where so many people he knew had been shot and killed, and a minute later pulled into the driveway while the sound system in the back of his trunk rattled the tinted car windows.

"Where is everyone?" he said to himself as he slammed his car door and walked toward the back of the ranch, carrying a box of black Compton Cowboys T-shirts for the parade. "I told everyone to be ready to go by ten a.m.!"

Randy's frustration with the group had been growing in recent months. Since he had assumed command of the Compton Cowboys and the ranch's day-to-day operations—making sure horse feed and material were purchased when necessary, and finding ways to raise money for the ranch—some were beginning to feel like he wasn't suited to lead the group. The bickering and talking behind his back were taking a toll on him. Sleepless nights quickly turned into moody mornings. Sometimes, when he was alone and out of sight of the group, the stress would overcome him, and he would have to fight back tears of frustration. It wasn't easy being the manager of the group and facing the pressure of losing the ranch.

Randy had fought hard to be able to get the cowboys to ride in this year's parade and reestablish the group as active members in the community by attending city council meetings and advocating for the rights of horseback riders in Compton. As Mayisha leaned closer into retirement, the ranch's youth program slowly began to dwindle, which left local youth with limited afterschool and weekend options. On top of this, assuming the responsibilities it took to manage the ranch would be challenging. Mayisha's commitment was matched only by decades of advocating for the Compton Jr. Posse, the organization she first started in 1988 as a way to provide Compton's youth with an alternative to gangs and violence. Filling her shoes seemed like a daunting task, but, like her, Randy was inspired to break age-old stereotypes about black cowboys and create opportunities for young children who were faced with the pressures of joining street gangs, as he once was.

At the same time, he wanted to create a new image for black riders in Compton that aligned with the experiences that he and members of the Compton Cowboys had been through. He wanted to make cowboy culture accessible and, most of all, cool.

"Carlton, go get your horse ready," Randy said as he made his way back inside the house. "I swear, you always messin' around." He continued to yell at his brother while slamming the back door loud enough for Byron to hear in the front of the house. "Always, always," he repeated.

"I done already took care of my horse," Carlton shouted. "We was out there early this morning! Don't be coming out here yelling at me like that, cuz!"

Byron stepped out of the back door and ignored the commotion.

"Aye, you got fifty cents?" he asked Randy.

"Not right now, man," Randy replied and continued walking. "Not right now, Byron."

Only seconds separated Randy and Carlton from birth, but the two couldn't have been more different. Randy was loud, gregarious, and comfortable in leadership roles. The sides of his head were closely trimmed, leaving only small Afro-textured hair on the top. Carlton preferred a calmer, quieter approach, often stood in the background, and wore his hair in dreadlocks. Whenever Carlton had a problem, Randy was there to help solve it through their daily bickering. One day it would be about finances, another it would be about punctuality or not asking permission to wear each other's hat. The quarrels never ended.

Keenan got dropped off in front of the ranch in a blue Toyota Camry at 10:40 a.m.—forty minutes after he was supposed to have been there. He was wearing a black cowboy hat and carrying a blue duffle bag that he carried close to his body. He had forgot some of his clothes at home and had hurried back to get them.

"Dang, you really are a cowboy," the Uber driver said as he waited for Keenan to get out of the car while looking at the horses in the stalls in the back of the ranch. "You wasn't lying."

Keenan smiled and shut the door behind in a hurry to get to the back of the ranch.

Charles arrived ten minutes later, wearing a black-and-white, baseball-style Compton Cowboys T-shirt, black tight-fitting jeans, and a new pair of Nike Air Jordans.

"How the heck did you get yours already?" Keenan asked as Charles approached him in the back of the ranch.

"Oh, this little thing?" He brandished a full-toothed grin and chuckled, pointing down at his T-shirt. "Man, you know I got the plug. I stay lookin' fly."

Randy sat down and texted everyone in the group chat. "WHERE Y'ALL AT?" he wrote. "Y'all were supposed to have been here at 10 a.m."

At the current rate, four out of ten cowboys wouldn't be enough to fill a riding line. It worried Randy. He feared that he and his friends would be the laughingstock of the parade, a far cry from the spectacular forty-person marches the Compton Jr. Posse used to put on every year.

This was the part of the job that he hated the most. Since their days as members of the Akrites, the cowboys had always looked up to Randy for his leadership. When he went away for school, at Occidental College, he still continued to lead. Even as a graduate student at Cal State University Northridge, his friends relied on him for support. But sometimes being a member of the cowboys and their manager was difficult. It meant he had to be everyone's friend and their leader, which required making tough decisions from time to time. Half the battle was getting people to show up to rides and events on time. The other half was managing the multiple personalities in the group who sometimes clashed.

"We're always just one fight away from destroying all that we've built," he often said. "This ranch could all come crashing down."

Anthony arrived back at the ranch an hour later in a 1991 brown Ford truck that he had bought months ago from one his Mexican neighbors in the Imperial Courts housing projects. He called it his *paisa* truck—as Mexican men who wore traditional Mexican cowboy clothing were called in Compton, especially those who drove pickup trucks with gardening or construction equipment in their truck beds. Anthony preferred the comfort of his paisa truck over anything else. It was unassuming and helped him keep a low profile on the streets. With large rust stains throughout its exterior and sporting a large crack that spanned the entire front windshield, the truck was a far stretch from the flashy cars he used to drive in his twenties, but at this point in his life, it provided him with exactly what he needed and allowed him to drive safely to and from the ranch every day.

Like the horses that he rode that offered him protection from the police or local gangs, his truck offered him safety. The police would just drive on past, not bothering to consider the ragtag truck or the person inside it as a threat.

The parade was set to start in an hour, and there was still no sign of the rest of the group. Xavier, an alumnus of the Jr. Posse and friend of the cowboys, had shown up to ride with the cowboys at Randy's request. There were now six, still not the entire group but more than before. After deliberating, Randy decided it was time to ride out.

"The rest of the guys are going to have to meet us over there," he shouted to everyone as they brushed their horses and cleaned out horseshoes with metal hooks. "If we don't leave soon, we're going to be late," he said.

When the cowboys rode as children, eager parade attendees lined up on both sides of the streets to see them ride on Compton Boulevard. Those who weren't old enough to ride proudly carried the Compton Jr. Posse blue-colored flag in front of the group.

Both the cowboys and the city had almost completely transformed since then. The blue Jr. Posse color scheme was now replaced by black-and-white, Old English–style writing with more flare and swagger. The shirts on their backs read *COMPTON COWBOYS*.

As the new generation of riders, looking good was a big part of the cowboy lifestyle that they hoped to create. Mayisha's dream of developing sharply dressed cowboys didn't always align with the vision they had for themselves. Some of them thought they were being forced to dress like squares. Now they had the option of dressing like traditional cowboys, but most of them enjoyed the freedom of riding in Nike Air Jordans, Gucci belts, and other designer clothes. Both their clothes and their horses became the armor that protected them.

Everyone's armor looked differently in Compton. The Campanella Park Pirus, a westside Compton Blood gang, wore red bandanas, draped softly on the side of their shoulders, and yelled out phrases like "suwuu" at any given moment. The red armor they wore both stopped and attracted bullets. The Acacia Blocc Crips from the westside yelled out words like "owiee, owiee" as a rallying call to both friends and foes. The color of their armor was dark blue.

Most people in the city of Compton, however, were not affiliated with gangs. Their color was that which they had been born into, the delicate black and brown skin that stood between them and the world. This, too, was armor.

Keenan and his horse Sonny were the first pair to make

their way out of the ranch's gates and onto Caldwell. Wearing a crisp black cowboy hat, dark sunglasses, tight-fitting black jeans, and black boots, Keenan looked as ready to step onto a western movie set as he did to ride in a family Christmas parade. The white T-shirt that he wore that morning was replaced by a large black CC shirt that clung close to his body. His hair was pulled back into two large braids that tightly gripped his scalp and tied together by two small purple rubber bands. Only small traces of the dry white flakes that his eczema skin condition produced on his skin showed on his scalp. Except for his hands, every part of his entire body was covered by black clothes, revealing multiple tattoos on the hands and fingers that clung to Sonny's reins.

Caldwell's street residents stood outside their homes as the cowboys made their way out to the street. One by one, they trotted—like they had done for years—past the safety of the ranch's black gates that separated them from the outside world.

"I'm so happy y'all are back," one woman said to Carlton as she stood on the street with bright green rollers on her head. "It brings me so much joy to see y'all again." It had been almost fifteen years since the cowboys last rode in the parade, and the same neighbors who had watched them as children were now snapping photos and videos with their cell phones. One boy approached the cowboys and took a selfie video. "I'm with the Compton Cowboys, y'all!" he yelled into his phone several times before finally walking away.

As more and more people gathered on the street to take photos with the cowboys, Sonny began to feel anxious and almost jerked Keenan off his back. Five years ago, a plastic gun had gone off near his head, and the fear of that day had stayed with him years later. Every time he heard a sharp sound, he'd slip into a state of panic. Keenan understood Sonny's trauma because he had also lived through some of it himself. Loud, sharp sounds also made him feel uneasy and anxious; they reminded him of the gunshots he and his friends had fled from on numerous occasions and the gunshots that took his old horse's life when he was in high school.

"Whoooa, Sonny," he whispered into his ear as an unknown car drove past the ranch playing loud rap music. "It's okay, you're safe with me."

Charles was the last cowboy to ride out of the ranch. He refused to wear a cowboy hat and boots, choosing instead to wear a new pair of Air Jordans and a black L.A. Dodgers hat. It was a far cry from the traditional dress he was forced to wear as an English-style jumper during competitions: britches, riding helmet, and long black show boots. When Mayisha had switched the program's style of riding from western to English years ago, Charles was the only member of the group who fully embraced it.

As the riders all waited in front of Louie's house, the adoring fans who had gathered to take photos made their way inside their homes to prepare for their own participation in the parade. Louie stepped out on the porch and looked at the group of children he had helped raise. As Randy and Carlton's single father, being a parent extended beyond raising his own two children. All the members of the Compton Cowboys had spent days and nights in his home as children. They shared countless meals and went on vacations and camping trips together. Being black cowboys was as much about riding as it was having a community where you could be your unapologetic self, and he helped provide that.

Louie wore his Occidental College T-shirt that morning with pride, proud of the only son of his to have graduated from college. The sight of the cowboys in front of his home brought emotions that he hadn't felt in years. He saw boys he had spent countless hours driving to and from rodeo circuit competitions. Some of them now had their own families to look after, but though they were much older and had more facial hair now, they would always be the same boys he remembered. He grabbed his phone from his pocket and took a photo to preserve the memory. The last time they rode together in the parade as teenagers, part of him believed that the legacy of black cowboys would end on the farms. But seeing them together again brought him to tears. He was filled with emotion, hopeful of the future in spite of the impending changes that the ranch was experiencing.

"Let's ride," Randy said while fixing the brim of his black

Stetson cowboy hat. "Yaaaa! . . . Yaaaa!" he yelled at his horse.

Randy, Carlton, Anthony, Keenan, Charles, and Xavier trotted down the street on their horses. The sound of their horses' hooves blended in with the other sounds on the farms, coming together in a synchronized, orchestral fashion, a series of rhythms that ended in a dramatic crescendo—a 'hood symphony, of sorts. The other Cowboys—Terrance, Layton, Tre, and Keiara—ended up needing to work and couldn't take the day off. Kenneth would be joining them later that day. The sounds of their horses repeatedly clicked on the street, reminding them of their days as members of the Jr. Posse. Mayisha used to lead the way and wear a long dark blue or orange African kente dress while she rode her horse. The posse trailed behind her, listening to her every command. "Paraaaaaaade, march!" she would yell to get the group going.

As they approached the intersection of Tichenor and Oleander, every block elicited a different memory for each rider. Some were joyous, some weren't. These were the same streets they had grown up riding on, and riding together reminded them of the days when their entire lives revolved around horseback riding—things seemed so much simpler then for everyone in the group.

Anthony thought about the time he had spent incarcerated and got flashes of the horse paintings that had given him something to look forward to. Keenan thought about Flower and the many parades they rode in together before she was killed. Randy thought about the dreams his father had about black cowboys and how he had always wanted his sons to have positive images of black cowboys in ways that he never had growing up. Charles thought about the example he could set for his children and hoped they never had to grow up in the same conditions that he did. Horses, he believed, could save their lives.

In one home, a group of twelve middle-aged Mexican men stood on horses wearing matching brown leather vests that read *Los Rancheros de Compton*. They gathered outside one of their members' homes, mounted on well-tamed Friesian horses. When someone's cell phone played Northern Mexican banda music—a music associated with brass instruments with rapid instrumentation—the horses danced on command.

Los Rancheros were a Mexican riding group from the farms who had been in the area for years. They had ridden with the cowboys in past parades and were friendly with them. When they arrived in the early 1980s, they were a minority, as the farms were composed entirely of black cowboys and riders. The rancheros were a part of waves of Mexican immigrants who left rural farm life in Mexican states like Jalisco and Michoacán with the promise of providing more for their families than life in Mexico could. They pooled their money together by living in multifamily homes and bought property, creating semblances of the lives they left behind. Many of the Mexican families who migrated to the farms often settled in contentious blocks and experienced the crime and violence of the crack-cocaine era of the 1980s and early 1990s.

This was also an era when many black families—some of them middle-class —were forced out of the farms because of increasing rents and the continued threat of violence. Some of them took their horses with them, choosing to resettle in cities around Los Angeles like San Bernardino, Fontana, and Moreno Valley, where they established new black horseback-riding communities. Since then, Compton's Latino population had increased to almost 70 percent of the entire city.

"Hola, amigos!" Keenan yelled out to the group of riders. "Que onda? What's up?" he asked as they greeted one another.

"Buenos días, Keenan," one of them replied.

Los Rancheros were accompanied by one of their children, who rode alongside them on a white pony with his father closely behind. "Espérame, Papa!" he yelled to his father as the group began to leave him.

When finding common ground between African-Americans and Latinos proved challenging for local politicians, the act of riding horses helped people come together.

The Compton parade was one of the only times when the entire city of Compton would unite under various affiliations and organizations. On the streets, both Crip and Blood gangs declared truces during the parade to allow people to safely attend the festivities. The truces ensured that local marching bands from high schools like Compton High and Compton Centennial could compete for bragging rights: the best performance was given an unofficial award that would last until the next year's parade.

Back in the Compton Jr. Posse days, the parade also required hours of committed and often strenuous practice that took place in front of the ranch on Caldwell. Mayisha had always circled the date on the calendar—the parade was an opportunity to show the city the effort her riders were putting into a noble cause: horseback riding. Practice usually began about one month before the parade and lasted two to three hours after school every day. Sometimes they would practice on horseback, but most of the time they were relegated to practicing without horses on the street. They marched in unison in rows of two. The children who weren't old enough to ride walked in front carrying Jr. Posse flags. "Remember to keep your back straight, smile, and wave with one hand and keep your other hand on the reins," the cowboys recalled Mayisha telling them when they were children. "We're setting an example to the whole city, so be at your best, you hear?" Moments before the parade would start, she'd turn to her riders and remind them: "Don't be acting a fool."

Still, the group had gotten significantly smaller since their youth, and fear of the future crept into their minds as they continued to ride toward the parade starting point on Compton Boulevard. As many as twenty to thirty riders rode back then, but today the number was fewer than ten. As children, many of them enjoyed riding in the parade, but as teenagers, they'd stopped because they felt dressing up like cowboys would hurt their image in school. Cowboys weren't the cool kids on campus, according to Randy and Carlton, but because they were Mayisha's nephews and next-door neighbors, they were forced to ride in the early stages of high school. The other cowboys believed that riding horses wouldn't help their dating lives because the girls they knew were interested in dating only athletes or gangsters.

The cowboys were riding past Compton High School's light blue walls when Anthony began recording the ride on his cell phone and shouting out to friends of his.

"What up!" he yelled to a carful of friends. "You see us!"

A silver early 2000s BMW sedan, with unmarked license plates, pulled up to the group from its rear. The sound of its loud rap music caused everyone—including the horses—to immediately turn around.

It was Rambo, Charles's younger brother.

"What's up, man!" he yelled as his slender body stuck out

of the window. He playfully threw up the Grape Street Crips gang sign to Charles amid the sounds of Young Dolph playing loudly from inside his car. "Y'all ready for the parade?"

"Hell yeah, man," Charles said, while others from the group greeted Rambo and also nodded in agreement.

"We ready," Anthony said, overenunciating the end of the word.

Rambo had also grown up with the group as a member of the Jr. Posse but had chosen gangbanging over horses as a teenager. Unlike his brother, Rambo ended up choosing the streets and was jumped into the Grape Street Crips. He was frequently in and out of prison, but still associated with the Posse, even though he hadn't ridden in more than fifteen years.

Rambo drove along the left side of the group and turned up his music, providing a lively soundtrack while he simultaneously live-streamed the ride on his phone.

"You see us!" he yelled at the top of his lungs for his social media followers. "We're the Compton Cowboys!"

The group was slowly increasing in size. Minutes after Rambo started to trail the group, another rider named Eugene, a twelve-year-old who was the youngest of the cowboys, caught up to the group riding a short-haired brown pony.

"Put this on," Randy said as he tossed Eugene a CC shirt.

"Thanks, man," he said with a big grin on his face.

Eugene had dreamed of being able to wear the black-and-white Compton Cowboys T-shirt that he had seen the guys wear during their rides. Like many of the cowboys, he also came from a generation of black cowboys who had deep roots in the South.

Anthony rode past the gas station on Alondra and Acacia with a heavy heart. His best friend, Black, had been shot and killed there six years prior. Black had introduced him to Mayisha and first encouraged him to ride horses as a child.

They rode past the Compton Courthouse, where many of them had been charged with crimes as minors and adults. They rode past the mural of a jubilant and toothy-grinned newly elected president Barack Obama on the side of the Compton Courthouse, which, at this point, was more satirical than an actual representation of the state of the city: the hope Obama had promised never quite found its way to the "hub" city between 2008 and 2016, as high murder rates and unemployment never changed.

Kenneth finally appeared on Ebony, a black Tennessee walking horse, moments before the parade began. His dreads hung below his black Stetson hat. His Compton Cowboys T-shirt squeezed his torso. As the group was slowly ushered in line toward the starting point, each cowboy seemed to be lost in his own thoughts.

The group turned their reins to the left and began trotting

on Compton Boulevard as soon as the parade conductor signaled them to move.

"Stay close to each other, y'all!" Randy shouted. "Two per line, two per line."

Randy found himself echoing the same words that Mayisha had once shouted to them as teenagers. Her influence was never too far away. "Bring up the line!" he yelled.

Crowds stood on both sides of the empty boulevard to watch them ride. They rode with elegance and assertiveness, carrying on the legacy of Compton's black cowboys who had been around since the 1950s. They rode past Long Beach Boulevard, Poinsettia, Sloan, and Burris, waving at people on both sides of the streets. It was the first time many of the horses had been in the parade, and the sounds of the streets, people, and music made some of them feel uneasy. Anthony carefully tugged on his horse Koda's reins and slowly withdrew from the group as people on both sides of the street waved at the cowboys. Anthony waved and smiled back.

The black families who had filled the streets during this youth had now been almost entirely replaced by brown faces. The stores and fast-food restaurants had remained, but black families who had made the Christmas parade a staple in their lives had been replaced by people he didn't recognize. The Compton he had once known had changed dramatically since his days with the Jr. Posse.

The cowboys approached the main stage, where an announcer held a microphone connected to a loudspeaker, acknowledging the groups that had participated in the day's events.

"Everyone ride in a straight line!" Randy yelled as they neared the stage. "Let's show them what we got."

And the group lined up just so.

The crowd's cheers intensified. Every cowboy felt something different, but they each knew that riding together was the one thing that had preserved their friendship throughout the years. Through the quarreling and confusion and deaths of friends and family, they continued to ride. It was the glue that kept them together. And they were the glue that kept their community together.

Eugene looked around in astonishment as he rode in his first-ever parade. Keenan stared long and hard at him and thought about the innocence he saw on Eugene's face, remembering his own innocence and the first time he rode in the parade.

At twelve, Eugene was too young to understand what life had taught Keenan as a twenty-seven-year-old black man in the city of Compton: the world would never fully accept the sight of black people on horses—and not only that, but the world would do everything in its power to keep him off his horse. Keenan wanted Eugene to understand the privilege of entering a lineage of black cowboys in Compton that had existed long before he was born.

Keenan wanted to tell Eugene that he hoped he never strayed too far away from his horse. He wanted to grab Eugene by the shoulders, look him in the eyes, and tell him that his horse could protect him. That his horse could, if he wanted, become a shield—a defense mechanism against injury in a city that would do everything in its power to penetrate it.

Keenan wanted to tell him these things, but he knew that Eugene, as he once did years ago, would have to learn on his own.

The announcer took the podium and began to read: "Ladies and gentlemen, straight out of the Richland Farms, the Compton Cowboys are alumni of the nonprofit youth organization the Compton Jr. Posse, which uses horses to keep kids off the streets."

The cowboys trotted past the stage, waving proudly at their city and receiving the loudest applause of the day. The brown faces in the audience cheered because they had never seen black cowboys before. The black faces cheered because it had been years since they had. The cheers forced smiles from the edges of each cowboy's mouth as they rode west on Compton Boulevard, toward the farms, toward the fading sun.

# THROUGH HER EYES

**MAYISHA BACKED HER WHITE CHEVROLET** Silverado pickup truck out of the driveway the same way she had done thousands of times over the past thirty years. She looked behind her right shoulder, put her arm on the passenger seat, and pushed the gas pedal slowly. After nearly missing Anthony's truck by inches on her way out, she switched gears, put her truck into drive, and moved forward while listening to R & B.

Medium height with light chestnut skin and a full build, Mayisha wore a long, full-body, relaxed-fit multicolored dress. The shiny metal band on her left wrist shone brightly in the sun while her left arm hung freely on the outside of her door as she made her way west on Caldwell in the direction of the hardware store. She passed a series of trucks that were parked on both sides of streets made only for vehicles and horses. Heavy-duty trucks like hers were a staple on the farms—they made transporting large machinery and pulling horse trailers easy.

Mayisha had tried different hairstyles over the years, but at this point in her life her hair was in thin, tightly coiled dreads that stretched down to her shoulders and were easy to manage. The reflection of her face on the driver's-side window was that of someone who was growing older. Her hair was almost fully gray, with a silver undertone that had replaced the dark black hair that she had been known for through the years. She paused to look at her own reflection in the mirror one last time before focusing her eyes on the road ahead.

It was only a few days before her retirement party, and there was still a lot of work to do on the ranch. A group of her closest friends had taken the responsibility of organizing the entire party, but Mayisha could not bear the thought of not being able to help out with her own party, so she did what she had always done best—she worked. After all, the party was going to be on her ranch, and as long as she was still a part of the organization, she would ensure that it ran as smoothly as possible. This was the same spirit that made her one of the most successful black women real estate agents in Los Angeles during the 1990s. It was the same spirit that helped create one of the first black-owned horse ranches in the United States.

Earlier in the year, after much speculation and a series of health problems, Mayisha decided it was time to hand over the reins of the ranch to her nephew Randy. Taking control of the ranch had always been a priority for Randy. As one of the few college-educated cowboys, he understood that leading the ranch required more than just the ability to teach youth how to ride horses. It also required becoming a leader in the community, which was something Mayisha had excelled at for the last thirty years. The ranch, in many ways, sustained the spirit of the community. If things weren't going well at the ranch, then chances were things wouldn't be going well in the community.

It was more than just horses for the cowboys. Losing the ranch would mean losing an important part of the ecosystem of the community. It was a place to train and ride horses, sure, but more importantly, it was a place where they could *belong*. The ranch was home to a series of interweaving relationships that they each called home. It functioned like a life source where emotional pain could be reconciled with the joy of riding horses. It was where friendships were preserved, where Anthony and Keenan first learned about the legacy of black cowboys. And now, if things went as they hoped, they were in a position to pass on that tradition to the next generation.

Over the years, the ranch had been kept alive through different income streams. Its board members, many of them wealthy white businesspeople, kept the ranch going with their generous donations, public and private grants, and scholarships through a network of like-minded benevolent sponsors. Mayisha succeeded at promoting her organization to wealthy celebrities in Los Angeles, like Magic Johnson and a host of others who had supported her over the years. Her vision for the ranch was directly linked to the vision for her community. Getting kids on horses, she believed, dramatically lowered the chances for gang involvement. Her model worked. It helped young people perform better in school by incentivizing them with rides and trips in and around Los Angeles. Horses also helped young people heal from different forms of trauma, and equine therapy became an informal tool to help children become softer, more compassionate members of the neighborhood.

When the cowboys officially banded together in 2016, they did so after years of being apart. Life had gotten in the way of the bonds that they formed as children, and many of them stopped coming to the ranch. Randy had moved out to the San Fernando Valley, where he was attending graduate school and living with Marriah, the mother of his child. Layton had been living in the neighborhood but only occasionally came around to the ranch, whenever Randy came back in town to visit. Tre had been competing professionally throughout the United States and excelling as one of the nation's best bareback riders and rodeo competitors. Keenan was working as a sous-chef at a restaurant near downtown Los Angeles, Charles was show jumping, and Kenneth was going on occasional rides through the neighborhood. Keiara, still battling the loss of her brother and horse, had taken a break from riding.

Forming the Compton Cowboys became a way not just to ride together again, but also to give back to the community that had raised them.

Some of the cowboys recognized that it wouldn't be an easy transition. Keenan worried the most. He understood that taking over the ranch would require a crash course on finances, outreach, and civic participation. The cowboys would have to find an entirely new board, since the older board members were also retiring.

In other words, taking over the ranch would require finding either a group of wealthy people to help fund the operation or other income revenue streams. The ranch cost at least twenty thousand dollars per month to run. Horse feed, veterinary checkups, and rent were expensive, and as more horses were donated to the ranch, the costs to keep them there went up. At the beginning of the year, when Keenan was asked to become one of the board members, he was unemployed and had just been fired from working as a chef at a restaurant in Los Angeles. He was cooking part-time and making dishes at home that he could sell to friends and family to make extra money. Saying yes was a big undertaking, and it was growing by the day. For the cowboys, and Keenan especially, it felt like a make-or-break situation. Either they were going to rally together and find ways to keep the ranch economically stable, or they would lose the ranch and the community that had been built around it for decades.

The biggest hurdle was themselves and the things they were dealing with internally, what Keenan called a "crabs-in-a-bucket mentality," meaning a struggle for survival that forced people to see one another as competition in situations where working together would have produced a much more favorable outcome. In Compton, it was both love and hate that drew people together. You were bound by blood, but blood didn't always guarantee love. The systems that were created around the cowboys were designed to see spaces as territorial, and each other, in the worst-case scenarios, as enemies.

Since the cowboys reunited almost four years ago, some issues had only exacerbated Keenan's worries. The brotherhood that they shared since they were children was durable. It was built on a sense of trust in knowing that the others would die for you. But in recent years, adulthood had gotten in the way. Tre and Charles had a fight that put a damper on their bond, and their stress and worry sometimes turned into shouting matches with the capacity to turn physical.

During the transition, when a few of the cowboys would get hired for commercial advertisements with brands, questions about money and exposure arose in ways they never had before. Some cowboys believed in giving back to the ranch, while others had to provide for their families. Kenneth became one of the most sought-after cowboys for shoots and bragged about it on social media.

While the year had brought the cowboys more notoriety for their commercial appeal—the sight of black cowboys was as jarring as it was enticing for brands—it also brought increased visibility to the ranch. New people were hanging out at the ranch, bringing the streets into the arena.

Rashid, Mayisha's oldest son, an older member of the Farm Dog Crips and one of the first to ride on the farms, had moved into Mayisha's home when she moved out. As an older member of the ranch, he often felt the responsibility of protecting the ranch despite pleas from Randy and his father not to. He had worked as the ranch hand before Anthony was released, but in recent years he had dedicated his life to becoming a traveling electrician. The cowboys respected him. After all, he was one of the 'hood's last original gangsters and family.

But his involvement and presence on the ranch also slowed down their plans. It was challenging for him to see the cowboys as adults. In his eyes they were still the same children he helped raise and bullied. Getting him to let go was one of the cowboys' biggest concerns.

As the cowboys planned for the transition, Mayisha continued to worry about the images that the cowboys presented. She was concerned that they would be seen as gangsters and not cowboys. At the same time, her actions sometimes negatively impacted the cowboys' hopes to keep the future of the ranch alive. She and Randy were often at odds about the direction for the ranch.

But if anyone understood Mayisha, it was Randy. He knew her motivations, how much the ranch meant to her, and how difficult it must be for her to know its fate was not entirely secure. She'd been at the helm for so many years and created everything the cowboys had, but at the same time, Randy recognized that she had the power to knock it all down herself if she wanted to. Getting Mayisha to let go of her control was one of the hardest challenges. The ranch was like her child, now thirty years old, and who wants to let their child go?

Being at the helm of the ranch operations and organization was something Randy had wanted for nearly his entire life. The ranch meant everything to him, and he had witnessed other people run the organization before who didn't have the same connection as he did. A year before the ranch was to be handed over to Randy, a Latino man was hired to run the organization. After a year, the man left amid disagreements over the vision for the ranch. The departure left Randy with a bad taste in his mouth. The guy never had a chance, Randy felt, and it had to do with rootedness. How does an outsider come in and deal with Compton? How does someone who's never set foot on Compton turf expect to transition young hoodlums into thriving citizens? Randy understood that you had to be from the 'hood, to have grown up in the 'hood, to make that change. And who was better suited for that than he was?

As Mayisha's retirement approached, Randy began to learn about the financial realities of the ranch. In a few months, without the prospects of new funding, the ranch would have to close and the community that the cowboys had created over the years could also come to an end. His aunt's retirement wouldn't mean only the end of her reign, it could also mean the board and funding streams would end. The thought crept closer as each day passed. If Mayisha and the community of supporters who worked with her left, then it was likely many funding streams would dry up as well. That's why it was important that they had confidence in the cowboys moving forward and in his leadership.

Keeping the ranch alive without the help of donors was a dream of Randy's. Mayisha had created a model that was easy for wealthy donors to buy into, and support had helped sustain a youth equestrian program for young black children in one of the most impoverished cities in the United States.

When the Compton Cowboys took over, however, almost

an entire generation had transpired. These weren't the children of yesteryear. The boys who had grown up going to the donors' homes to learn how to ride and spend time in communities outside Compton had turned into black men who were living different lives.

Young black men at the helm of the ranch operation instilled doubt, worry, and fear in the hearts of many of the donors. They doubted their ability to continue the ranch, and Mayisha's concerns only compounded their own. Their lack of support began to show as each day passed. It felt like the world was against them, but if the ranch was going to survive, it was going to be up to them.

A few weeks later, a large outdoor tent that covered most of the riding arena was being installed all morning by five men who worked tirelessly to make sure it would be up before the end of the day. They had been working for hours until one of them realized that some of the support ropes were missing. The fiasco had halted progress, and several of them sat down and listened to music on their phones. After an hour and various phone calls, another worker decided to head back to the office to pick up the ropes that should have been brought that morning.

*None of that would have happened on my watch*, Mayisha thought to herself while observing the entire thing from the driver's seat of her truck earlier that morning.

As the founder and director of the Compton Jr. Posse for

the past thirty years, she had run the organization by using a combination of tough love mixed in with sporadic moments of tenderness and affection that were felt but rarely seen. Her brand of tough love was often the only defense against the neighborhood gangs that she was in competition with for new recruits throughout the years. She had to provide the same things they did in order to keep children interested—in other words, a sense of belonging.

Mayisha was also in competition with the impact of a rap group that made recruiting horseback riders challenging. The rise of Compton gangster rap group N.W.A, consisting of Eazy-E, Dr. Dre, DJ Yella, and MC Ren, natives of Compton and South Central, helped usher in a new image for Compton while she was opening the ranch. When she tried to keep her kids off the streets by preaching the gospel of horseback riding, the messages of songs like "Gangsta Gangsta" promoted the life that she was fighting against.

If Compton was already stigmatized around the world as a haven for crime and violence, N.W.A further crystalized deep-seated fears of gun-toting young black youth who—because of limited economic and social opportunities—took matters into their own hands. None of this made Mayisha's job any easier. The children of the neighborhood had to decide between the version of Compton that N.W.A was creating and the Compton she wanted to create. It was a battle that she often lost.

She continued to drive toward the hardware store in search of an assortment of rocks to fill up the fifty glass vases that she had purchased to place on the tables. The party also required palm trees to go along with the theme.

It would be their very last time at the ranch for a lot of her friends and family. The same people who had helped her accomplish her dream of maintaining one of the only black ranches west of the Mississippi—a reliable team of donors, philanthropists, and community leaders—were also aging and running out of the energy and resources to keep the ranch afloat.

Since she had moved away to Norco a few years before, her connection to the ranch had changed. Fewer children showed up to learn how to ride on the weekends, and the program that she started for her children and their friends began to lose its allure.

Driving through the farms only confirmed what she already knew: the community had drastically changed since she first moved to Caldwell Street over thirty years ago. The sight of black children and families who played in the streets and walked to and from local schools had been replaced by Latino schoolchildren who walked in groups of at least five or six with young mothers who pushed strollers and walked close behind them. Even the black waste collectors who had picked up the ranch's trash were replaced by brown faces.

As a former real estate broker, Mayisha understood the

housing market and why African-American families had begun to move out. As more and more African-American families moved to cities like San Bernardino, Fontana, and Ontario, Mexican families began moving in and living in homes together so they could afford the rising housing costs. Single families often could not bear the prices, but multiple families and multiple incomes could. Some Compton residents, and local public officials, saw this as an attempt to force black families out of the community, which created racial rifts that began at the political level and eventually trickled down to schools.

Taco Tuesday wasn't a day when people ate Mexican food in Compton. For many years, it meant the day of the week when black teenagers would pick fights with Mexicans on schoolyards throughout Compton. Punch-a-Mexican Friday was also a popular day.

Even as a staunch pro-black thinker and supporter of the Nation of Islam, Mayisha never subscribed to the politics of division that plagued her community. She understood the factors that drove Latino families out of countries like Mexico and led them to settle in Compton. She created the Jr. Posse for the children of the farms, and as time passed, that naturally meant more Latinos.

"Where's your father?" Mayisha asked a Latino teenager who was helping load up the back of a truck with brown dirt in front of Jose's house. She put her truck in park and waited on the right side of the street. "He said on the phone earlier today that he would be here to help me get some palm trees."

The boy stopped what he was doing and walked into the house to look for Jose.

Moments later, the front door swung open and Jose stepped out with a phone next to his ear, wearing a blue T-shirt and gray work pants with different-colored paint on them. His scruffy demeanor was balanced out by a pleasant smile.

"Hola, Mayisha," he said. He placed the phone by his side without hanging up.

"How are you, Jose?" Mayisha asked in a joyful tone from the inside of her truck. The old friends hadn't seen each other since she moved to Norco, a community located fifty miles east of Compton. They had worked together and for each other on numerous occasions throughout the years. Seeing people like Jose reminded her of the beauty and hardship that had come with the organization she founded. The success of the ranch was as much about Mayisha as it was about the relationships she had formed with people like Jose who lived on the farms. They were built on respect and trust and guided by a language of love.

"Well, I came here for those palms that we spoke about on the phone this morning. If you happen to find any, bring them over to the ranch. I have to go buy dirt for some vases right now, but just drop them over there if you find any.

"And come to my party, your whole family is invited," she added while putting her car in gear and beginning to drive off.

"Okay, Mayisha, that sounds good," he said. "I'll let you know what I find." He returned to a conversation on his phone, seamlessly switching back into Spanish.

As she began to shift her car into drive, an older-model Chevy Camaro coming from the opposite direction drove up to the left side of her car playing loud Mexican banda music. A long metal crutch hung from the window.

"Is that you, Guero?" Mayisha said as the car drove up next to her.

"Hi, Mayisha. You like my music? It's your CD!" exclaimed a fair-skinned Mexican man with blue eyes. He was holding on to his crutch with one hand and the steering wheel with the other. His daughter sat in the passenger seat and looked down at her phone while the loud music blared out of his speakers and into the neighborhood.

"That is not my music, man!" she said with a large smile, followed by a short laugh. "You're crazy!"

Guero spoke to Mayisha about a five-year-old mare that he could not ride anymore since she had broken her leg a few months ago. "I'll sell it for a few hundred," he said. "I don't care, I just want to get rid of it."

Mayisha agreed to ask around to see if anyone was interested.

"Take your CD before you go," Guero said as he ejected the Mexican banda CD and handed it to Mayisha.

As she took the CD and placed it on her dashboard, she said, "Bye, Guero!"

Jose and Guero had been her friends for years. When she needed sand for her stalls and they had extra, they would drop it off at the ranch free of cost. When she had extra sand, she would do the same for them. Every horse-owning family on the farms worked in synchronicity, regardless of their race. They were part of a unique horseback-riding community and understood only from inside the confines of the ranch.

Life had hardened some aspects of Mayisha, but if you caught her on the right day at the right time, you would find her laughing full-body laughs. It was part of the reason why people loved and trusted her. She had the ability to speak to anyone, and her close relationships with people throughout Compton were a testament to that.

Her hand remained outside the truck as she waved to pedestrians and cars alike. She knew most of them by their first names. Sometimes she would drive around and people would walk up to her and call her "Mom." She wouldn't recognize them at first, but then she would realize they were once a part of the CJP.

Besides the kinder version of Mayisha, there was also another side to her. Her role sometimes required a sterner approach than she would have liked. Many of the children she brought to the ranch came from broken homes. Responsibility and discipline were hard to come by and not readily enforced. She'd learned how to show kids tough love, knowing they wouldn't survive otherwise.

She expected excellence and a full commitment from each CJP rider in ways that some children could not bear, leading to frequent falling-outs with several children and families.

At one point she decided to switch up the riding styles and opted to leave western riding for English-style riding. Western saddles were heavier and larger than English saddles and were primarily designed as a way to spread the weight over a larger area of the horse, making longer rides more comfortable. English saddles, in contrast, were designed to give the rider closer contact with the horse when jumping.

But changing the style of riding did more than make riders adjust the size of their saddles. It eventually changed the demographics of the program.

Western-style riding provided an outlet for aggression and anger for many of the young people who rode with the Jr. Posse. Western riders rode fast and hard and prided themselves on their aggressive style. It was the same feeling that many of the youth felt after a big hit on the football field. At-risk youth were able to ride as fast and as freely as they wanted; it became an outlet and a form of therapy. When the styles of riding changed, that feeling was gone, and, as a result, so were most of the kids. They were asked to dress differently: denim jeans, white T-shirts, and cowboy hats were exchanged for black helmets, knee-high boots, dark jackets, and polo shirts. Some of the kids who needed the program more than anyone left after refusing to ride English and were eventually lost to the streets.

For Mayisha, changing riding styles had been incentivized by the prospect of securing more funding from wealthy donors. Western-style riding wasn't as lucrative as English was, and Mayisha believed that the ranch would be able to attract more donors and resources. She never imagined it would deter kids from joining. She never imagined it would be a life-or-death situation for some of her riders.

"Where is my wallet?" Mayisha said to herself. She was frantically searching through a pile of receipts and empty coffee cups inside her truck while parked inside the McDonald's drive-thru. Her truck was a haven for miscellaneous items like receipts and paperwork that had piled up since she first bought it.

"There it is." She leaned out the window to speak into the drive-thru intercom. "I'll have two burritos and a coffee, please."

At this point in her life, her health was failing. She had gained some weight and was no longer the young, vibrant, energetic woman that she had been required to be most of her life. Running the ranch had taken a deep toll on her body over time. Just two years earlier, she had suffered a mild stroke, leaving her bedridden for almost a month. She had since slowly eased her way into the background of the ranch's daily operations.

Like other black families during the World War II era, the Hook family arrived in Harbor City with the hope of working in war industry jobs available to African-Americans. They were lured from Oklahoma with the promise of a better life, a chance to live outside the bounds of racially restrictive communities. They believed in the dream of California, and Mayisha's mother found work as a cook for several healthy family initiatives, while her father, a World War II veteran, worked on the railroads after the war. When Mayisha graduated from Loyola Marymount University, she immediately began working in real estate. Her career advanced, and soon she was known as one of the savviest realtors in Los Angeles.

But while her career ascended, she felt like something was missing in her life. One day while scouting for properties, a client of hers recommended that she look at Richland Farms. There's farmland and horses, they said, and it's right in the middle of Compton. Raising her children near a big plot of land where animals roamed freely had always been a dream of hers. The stories her father had shared with her, vivid memories of his days as a child growing up on a farm in the Oklahoma countryside, flashed through her head.

She cherished memories of watching westerns with her

father every Saturday morning, but it also upset her that there were never black people in them. Her father would get so happy when the Native Americans would beat the white soldiers, feeling a sense of kinship or solidarity with them even though he was once in the military.

Like her, the children who showed up at Mayisha's makeshift ranch had never seen black cowboys on their television screens. They never read about the history of black cowboys in the founding of the American West. They were never taught about the ingenuity of cowboys like Nat Love, who was born a slave in Tennessee in 1854, freed at the conclusion of the Civil War, and gained prominence throughout the Southwest as a trusted guide and showman. Or about Bill Pickett, one of the West's most famous rodeo champions and actors who would later be inducted into the Pro Rodeo hall of fame. Cowboys, the children believed, were white and only looked like the cowboys they had seen, such as John Wayne or Clint Eastwood, both made famous in Hollywood films for their roles in western films that depicted them as victors in ruthless gunfights against Native Americans. So when young black children began to ride horses on Caldwell Street, it changed the neighborhood and their lives forever.

The new generation of cowboys, however, led by her nephew Randy, worried Mayisha. She had raised the cowboys under a strict code, through morals and ethics that she had learned when she first converted to Islam in the 1980s and began following the teachings of Minister Farrakhan of the Nation of Islam. Minister Farrakhan's message impressed her, and after meeting her first husband, she converted to Islam and changed her last name to Akbar.

Being a member of the Nation of Islam continued to guide her life years later, and the cowboys, she believed, were in danger of living up to some of the very stereotypes that she had tried so hard to combat.

She was concerned about her nephew's group now taking the reins of the ranch. They'd constantly tell her she was "old-school," but in her heart she felt some of the old ways were more wholesome. She needed them to understand how detrimental some of their changes were to their culture—black cowboy culture.

Her biggest concern for the eventual transition of the ranch was the way the cowboys carried themselves. As members of the Compton Jr. Posse, they were never allowed to ride in anything but the blue CJP shirts that they were given. They were never allowed to ride shirtless or with anything but crisp riding boots. Cowboys like Kenneth, notorious for riding without a shirt, had the ability, she believed, to undo much of the work that she had given so much of her life to create.

Still, while she had qualms about the direction that the cowboys were heading, she understood that in a few days the ranch would no longer be hers. It felt like letting a child go off to college for the first time and realizing the child might never return home again. Mayisha understood that her nephew and the guys who were working on the ranch had to take the reins, that she had to trust them to do a good job. But she hoped they would see the bigger picture, particularly when it came to how they would lead the next generation of kids.

She wished she'd never had the stroke—perhaps it would have allowed the Jr. Posse's board members to continue to believe in her ability to run the ranch the way she used to. They believed that the funding—almost thirty thousand dollars a month and extensive fund-raising—would be a challenge without her because Mayisha was a fearless fund-raiser. On top of an uncanny wit, it was her charm and ability to connect with people that proved effective.

But there was only one Mayisha, and finding someone to replace her was almost unimaginable. She often thought of the days when she first started the Compton Jr. Posse in 1988, and of how far they had come since: the sponsored trips for her riders around the world, the college scholarships that the organization provided, and the lives she had saved over the years. With her retirement, she decided to close the operation down for one year, until Randy started talking about how they could try to keep things going and potentially generate income for the organization with entertainment.

Mayisha had mixed feelings about the cowboys' reliance

on striking it rich through entertainment. She was no stranger to the entertainment industry, and she had been approached by production companies and Hollywood studios through-out the years to develop films about the CJP. The deals seemed lucrative, but she was more interested in preserving the integrity of the image. She worried that the cowboys had delusions of grandeur and didn't quite understand the nature of the entertainment business.

She tried to manage their expectations, tried to teach them the value of being patient and putting in the hard work—eventually the industry would come to them. If she'd learned anything as a handler of the ranch, it was that hard work was hard for a reason.

# THE FIRES

**WHILE CONCERNS ABOUT THE FUTURE** of the ranch continued to simmer on the farms, Charles Harris was able to momentarily escape them on his drives to his training sessions in Malibu.

He turned up the volume in his car a little louder than usual and played smooth R & B while the dark blue Pacific Ocean water reflected on the outside of the driver's-side door. To his right were the Santa Monica bluffs, one of the first places where he took the mother of his children on a date. A photo of Bayley and Blake, his two children, was attached to his dashboard with an old piece of gum. His kids were a reminder of why he was making the ninety-minute drive up the Pacific Coast Highway to Malibu in the first place.

The Pacific Coast Highway was busier than normal for a Thursday afternoon. The arduous drive from Compton to Malibu on a weekly basis had become routine for Felicia Jones's eldest son. He was the pride and joy of the family and an Olympic hopeful with big dreams. Training to become the first African-American Olympic hunter-jumper required hours upon hours of hard work and dedication. Since the beginning of the year, however, finding the time to jump didn't come as easy as it used to. Sponsors and supporters began to dwindle as the costs of competitive jumping events and training continued to increase.

What began as a daily drive to a donor's ranch in the Malibu hills declined to three times a week, and eventually to only one training session a week. The less time he spent training, the more weight he gained and the less smooth his jumps became. The timing that he had been known for in the equestrian community was slowly beginning to slip before his eyes.

On top of that, working as a part-time construction worker and a stocker at Walmart squeezed the minutes out of each of his days. Every hour that he clocked in to work felt like an hour that took him further away from the dream that he had first had when he began jumping as a fourteen-year-old.

At twenty-seven, the dream had seemed more unattainable than ever.

He pulled off the Pacific Coast Highway and made a right onto a dirt road that eventually led to Susan's ranch. She was a supporter of the Jr. Posse that he had known for years. His car tires skidded on the loose gravel, leaving a growing trail of dust behind as he continued driving up the mountain.

For someone who had been born and raised in Compton, driving through nature was cathartic and removed him from the dangers of his neighborhood. Every time he drove there, he was immediately transported into a world where wildlife outnumbered the humans and cars he was used to being around. It was an escape, a world that wasn't defined by the black-and-white uniforms of police officers. Or the black skin of young men in his neighborhood who were often shot at by the same police officers. This world was green. And its natural soundscape overpowered the sounds coming from his car's speakers and the low murmur of the cars of the Pacific Coast Highway miles below.

Susan's home was the farthest on the road, and getting there required driving on a number of dirt roads before reaching her property. The entrance felt familiar at this point. He had made the drive so many times before, it began to feel like muscle memory—the same way he used to shoot free throws with his eyes closed in high school to impress the prettiest girls on campus. Pulling off onto the dirt road was his favorite part of the drive because it allowed his mind to zone out and everything he worried about to disappear, while what mattered to him came into crystal-clear focus: his children, his family, and their future.

Charles parked his car, got out, and took a long whiff of the fresh Malibu air, picking up a scent of the gardenias and roses in the nearby garden.

"Hi, Charles," Susan said with a smile, welcoming him inside her home. "Are you hungry?" Charles smiled and said that he was.

It was routine for them to eat and study the equestrian books that she had bought for him years ago. He studied the books with an intensity that he never applied to his schoolwork. Studying diligently and reading about training methods from the best equestrian jumpers was the only way to improve his jumping, and there were tips in the book that he hadn't learned on the farms. An hour later, Charles and Susan headed down to the stables to groom and saddle up two Thoroughbred horses that poked their heads out from the stalls as they approached them. Warm Blood, Charles's favorite horse, neighed and flipped its tail at the sight of Charles and Susan.

Warm Blood stood still while Charles brushed his shaggy brown coat, occasionally flipping his mane in the air. He was one of the most beautiful horses Charles had ever seen, and his personality reminded him of other horses that he rode in

Compton throughout his life: kind, energetic, and warm. Charles had never owned his own horse, but grooming Warm Blood felt like the closest thing he had to it. "Good horse," he said. "Good horse." After thirty minutes, the two hopped onto their horses and rode around the local trails before training.

Although Charles's jumping timing had declined over the past year, the intensity that he brought to each of his training sessions hadn't. The first hour of training included flatwork—a series of slow trots over poles on the ground that loosened up the horses before jumping. "Groundwork," as Charles also called it, was as important as jumping because it let him feel out what mood the horse was in that day. If the horse was having a bad day, it would tense up when Charles pulled on its reins. If it was calm and rested, it would comply with each tug of the reins. The second hour included jumping and working on perfecting the two-point jumping position, known as a forward seat, which allowed riders to balance on the horse.

Charles crouched on his horse and got ready for the first big jump of the day. He bent his knees in a forty-five-degree angle and lifted his bottom off the horse's back as the horse timed its jump and sailed over the wooden bar with ease, landing moments later as Charles's body hovered closely over the horse's back.

He rode toward the next jump.

One stride, two strides, just like he had done for the past fifteen years of his life, and Warm Blood was in the air again. His body leaned forward on the second jump, prompting a response from Susan, who stood feet away.

"Make sure you let the horse's feet relax on the landing," she said while looking intently. "And keep your knees bent a little more next time."

As a jumper, it was Charles's job to ensure that his horse was comfortable with every jump. Horses like Warm Blood had been trained to jump their entire life and just needed the reassurance to make the jump. Charles admired the power of the horse when it approached the jump—he could feel the horse's strength building up, knowing the horse wanted to get over the jump. But it was important for him to keep rhythm with Warm Blood to help him make that jump, together.

He landed the rest of his jumps that afternoon, leaving a big smile of Susan's face.

Charles felt conflicted when news came that Mayisha would no longer be running the ranch at the end of the year. He had been one of CJP's most successful jumpers and one of the program's stars. When other members of the CJP pushed back against switching to English-style riding, Charles was one of the only riders who welcomed it with open arms. Mayisha was the first person to introduce him to show jumping and the first to help him realize that he could make a career out of it. But because show jumping required the most resources and training, Charles would have to find creative ways to fund his training. None of his closest friends knew how to ride English, so he had to rely on wealthy riders to show him the ropes—it would be his only hope for survival.

He was now a twenty-seven-year-old and the names and faces had changed, but the same wealthy white horseback riders continued to help. Each trainer had seen the same potential in him that led him to believe he could become an Olympian. But the same issues arose with nearly every single one of them. After a while, they all wanted to be compensated for their time and for using their horses. The promise of Charles striking it rich in a competitive show-jumping circuit wasn't enough for them to continue to support him.

But making the Olympics was still Charles's dream.

He really wanted to show kids from the 'hood that you didn't have to be a gangster or sell drugs. He remembered how in the early days of riding, he didn't want to wear his britches in public because he felt ashamed. It took years to shed that embarrassment. Now, after all these years of hard work, he didn't give a damn. Trainers might come and go, and horses, too, but he wore his britches every day. Being a rider was a part of him now.

Daily training at Susan's continued for the next few months. His timing was improving, and his landings, always his lowest set of scores, were smoothing out. The next competition was months away, and the progress he was making impressed everyone on the ranch.

One morning he received a call from Susan describing an issue that had recently arisen at her ranch. She explained that the property was in the middle of a tough legal battle with a pair of local residents who were concerned that the horses that she owned were damaging their property. The phone call was reminiscent of one that he received late at night the previous November when Nicole, one his trainers, called to explain that she could no longer train him because of her legal situation. Then there was a different trainer, who eventually told him he couldn't train with him anymore because his rate was too high and Charles could no longer afford him.

He hung up the phone with Susan and burst into tears. Just when all the stars began to point in his favor, when his timing was getting back to where it once was, something else had come up to destroy his plans.

As a black boy from Compton, wealthy white people with kind hearts had always taken a liking to Charles. They had been the reason for his development as a jumper since he first joined the CJP. He was their favorite. His full-toothed grin, handsome features, and pleasant disposition quelled any deep-seated fears they may have had about black people. Giving back to black boys and girls from the 'hood like Charles was a way to reconcile their thirst for charity and absolve themselves, he believed, from any sense of guilt they may have had about racism.

At the end of the day, they still had control over his dream and were armed with the power to take it away at any moment. He felt vulnerable, as though wealthy white people were toying with his life.

Driving back to the ranch after the call, he knew he needed to get more support. To find the right people to back him up. To find somebody, anybody, to believe in him enough.

When his Malibu trainer could no longer help him, it was the last straw for Charles. It also coincided with the troubles he had begun to experience with Koya, the mother of his two children. When the two had first met near the farms over seven years ago, they were instantly drawn to each other. After courting for a few weeks, they began dating and soon became inseparable. Charles loved that Koya lived down the street from the ranch. He could ride horses and see her on the same day. It was the perfect setup. But things changed after they had Bayley, their daughter, and then Blake. When they moved in with Charles's mother in Palmdale, Koya felt isolated from her family and friends in Compton despite the lower cost of living. As months passed, they began to spend more time apart than together.

A few years later, they were fully separated and living in different parts of the city. Koya had filed to have full custody over Bayley, who was now six, and Blake, who was four. In the meantime, Charles was allowed to see his children only on weekend custody visits. Now he was separated from his children and the horses that could provide for him and his family.

Court visits became the norm. During one visit, Charles lost control and began yelling at both Koya and the judge. He was later sentenced for contempt, but the charges were eventually dropped. The time that he did spend with his children was spent at malls and parks around the cities. Even if he couldn't see them as often as he would have liked, he was going to make sure they wore the nicest things. He bought Jordan basketball shoes and sweat suits that Charles believed Koya would return in exchange for money. To support himself and his family, he took a job at Walmart as an overnight stocker. A few months later, his brother, Rambo, joined him. Together, they unloaded pallets from trucks and stocked aisles with spatulas, knives, and coffeemakers from late at night into the early hours of the morning. It wasn't the life he had imagined for himself, but it kept him afloat and allowed him to purchase things for his children.

In November, months after Charles got Susan's call, months after he had begun thinking about making a comeback in the sport, he was flipping through the channels when he stumbled on news of a raging fire that was quickly spreading throughout Malibu—the same area that he had practiced in for the past few years. The fire had already killed two people and was on the path to destroying thousands of acres of land, charring and blackening the same soil that he had used to practice his jumping on. He watched the television as the fires burned, knowing that his dreams were also burning to the ground as more and more structures were destroyed. For a while, he had been meaning to call Susan, but without an arena to practice on, the phone call would be futile. If things had seemed bleak for Charles prior to the fires, his dream of becoming an Olympic champion seemed more unattainable now than ever.

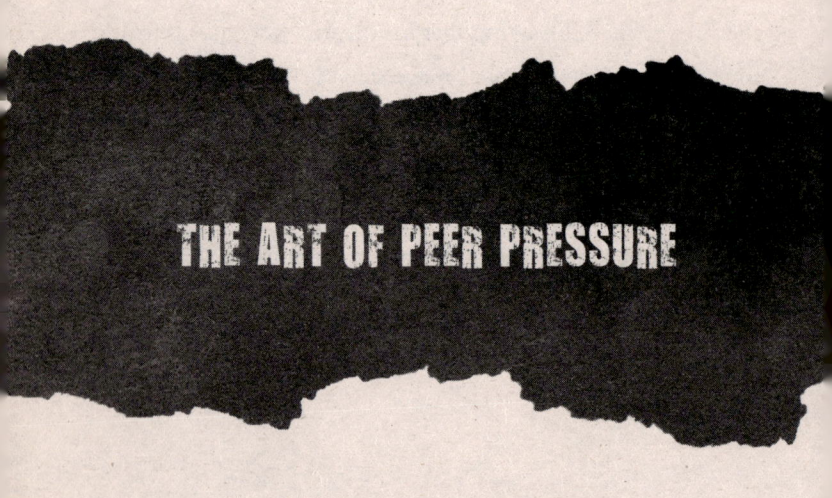

# THE ART OF PEER PRESSURE

**ONE OF BYRON'S SHOELACES** dragged closely behind him as he walked down Caldwell wearing a faded black T-shirt and baggy blue jeans. Tiny beads of sweat began to collect on his forehead as the sun beat down on his body. His eyes remained fixated on the ground beneath him, looking up only when a car passed him, hoping to see a familiar face inside.

In the old days, Byron would have recognized every car that drove down Caldwell, but with the changing of the neighborhood and his CD business gone, he hardly felt like he knew anyone now. The fast-paced Mexican music that played from inside most of the cars that drove up and down the farms was completely foreign to his ears, and it was only the Mexican horseback riders who had been friends with Mayisha who greeted him as they rode past on finely groomed white Friesians. The sound of their hooves faded away as they both walked in opposite directions.

Almost an hour earlier, a group of Mexican mothers had rushed their children to school wearing house slippers and sweatpants, hoping to beat the sound of the eight a.m. bell that signaled the start of their children's school day.

By the time they dropped their children off that morning, Byron had already been walking around the farms for a couple of hours.

He walked on Alondra Boulevard toward Acacia, stopping at the gas station to ask for change—the same gas station where Black, a childhood friend from the ranch, had been murdered years ago. "You got fifty cents?" he asked a few different people that morning. One person gave him a quarter, another a few dimes; most ignored him. After spending an hour there, he made his way to the canals to visit a group of homeless people he had befriended over the last few months.

Byron sat on an upside-down white bucket and watched the group while they drank out of brown paper bags near a batch of fresh horse hoof marks that members of the Compton Cowboys had left on the canal trail earlier that week. A few men sat with their backs against the wall, taking advantage of the shade it provided them from the harsh Compton sun.

One of the people in the group, a husky black man with a buried scar under his right eye, wore a two-toned durag on his head and was straightening out a blue tarp. He carefully draped it across two shopping carts filled with bottle cans and pieces of scrap metal that he had been collecting, forming a home encampment. A vintage light blue Compton High letterman's jacket with the name *Johnson* embroidered across the left breast—his most prized possession—lay on the ground, eagerly awaiting the return of the Friday night stadium lights that lit up his nearby alma mater once a week.

One of the women who had recently joined the group caught Byron's attention. She was white and from the Midwest and had spent years lost in the underworld of drug addiction in downtown Los Angeles's skid row. She had moved to Compton earlier in the year to follow a boyfriend, who had since abandoned her for another woman. The mysterious woman with wide Caribbean-blue eyes reminded him of some of the actresses in the old cowboy westerns that he had watched as a child. At one point during her youth the sun must have radiated against her long, healthy blond hair, but now her hair had become dull and lifeless from months without bathing. Byron shyly smiled at her while she sat next to the letterman's jacket, leaving Byron and the rest of the group alone with their thoughts.

Byron walked back to the ranch and arrived at the same

time as Layton, one of the Compton Cowboys, who parked his dark blue shiny Lexus sedan next to Anthony's truck, barely missing hitting the same mailbox that had been knocked down too many times to count over the years.

"Hey man, you g-g-got fifty cents?" Byron quickly asked Layton with an outstretched hand as he got out of his car.

Like the rest of the cowboys, Layton had known Byron his entire life and remembered the days when Byron would give him and his friends CDs or buy them sodas and candy from the convenience store. He never forgot these memories and was one of the only cowboys who almost always gave Byron money whenever he asked.

"What up, Byron?" Layton asked him, reaching into his pocket to grab a wrinkled dollar. He handed it to him.

Byron eyes widened as he grabbed the dollar. "Thanks, man," he said without a stammer as the two walked to the back of the ranch, where several of the cowboys had been hanging out. They walked to an area that hadn't physically changed as much as their bodies had in the last thirty years. The large riding arena, fifteen horse stables, and a thirty-foot-high barn were stacked with hay and ranch equipment. A trailer that hadn't been used in years now served as a storage space for reins and other tack. On one side inside the barn's walls were several dry-erase boards where Anthony was able to keep track of the horses' health and feeding times.

The group was celebrating Anthony's and Terrance's

birthdays, and several of the guys had gathered inside the
toolshed to listen to music and avoid the heat. Charles, the
group's jumper, and Carlton, Randy's twin brother, were
busy playing a dice game while Keenan watched diligently,
egging both of them on as the dice continued to roll different sets of numbers, prompting different responses from the
group.

"Snake eyes!" Charles yelled.

Anthony and Terrance sat back and watched the game
from nearby chairs. The pair had known each other for as
long as they could remember, and celebrating their birthdays
together had become tradition since Anthony was released
from prison more than twelve years ago. Though they were
both in their mid-thirties, the years had been extremely kind
to them. At thirty-six, only a few gray hairs had begun to
show on Anthony's head. Terrance, on the other hand, hadn't
changed much. He still had the same long, slender face and
dark brown skin free of wrinkles, continued to prefer the
flashy fashion choices that he had been known for on the
farms for years, and, at six feet six inches tall, was often mis-
taken for a basketball player.

They were the eldest of the group and had acted like mentors for a lot of the guys over the years. When disagreements
occurred, they were usually the first ones to settle them.
Both of them had been members of the Acacia Blocc Crips,
but at this point in their lives they weren't actively in the

gang, though still very much connected to the streets.

When they were born, the city of Compton was known as one of the world's most dangerous communities. Unemployment was almost twice the national average, and social and political neglect led to the rise of organized street crime and gangs throughout the city. Crime drastically increased, murder rates skyrocketed, and school systems nearly crumbled at the hands of mismanagement and as the allocation of resources shifted out of the city. Many of the middle-class black families who had formed the backbone of the city moved out, creating a "black exodus." By the mid-1980s, a drug epidemic had emerged, leaving a scathing effect on the city and all its inhabitants. Anthony and Terrance were both from this era and born into a generation where babies were often exposed to drugs as fetuses.

Layton wore a crisp Barcelona soccer jersey and a black baseball cap with white Apple earbuds in his ears. His beard had grown over the fall, and with winter approaching, there was more incentive to grow it out. Since he had begun to work at an electronic appliance store, he spent less time on the ranch than he had ever done. Earlier in the year, when his only source of income was producing beats for local rappers, he lived in between the Hook residence, a girlfriend's house, and with Kenneth, another cowboy, in his back house that doubled as a bedroom and makeshift recording studio. Layton's son, now in elementary school, lived close by and split time with the family of his mother, who had suddenly passed away years ago from a stroke in her sleep.

When he wasn't bragging about how much better a rider he was than everyone else in the group, Layton was quick to joke with everyone. Like Charles's, his jokes had no boundaries. Anyone could be a victim.

While the front of the ranch was quiet, the back of the ranch was buzzing with more energy than usual. Music blasted on the speaker system while Anthony and Terrance sat on oddly shaped chairs. As the eldest members of the cowboys, the two had survived some of its toughest times together. Through gang wars, dirt-bike-riding accidents, and the deaths of close friends, the two had an inseparable bond.

Terrance was the tallest member of the group and also its most reserved. He never really seemed rattled by anything. If the stereotype about people from the West Coast was that they were laid-back, he fit that bill perfectly. He spoke slowly and with a slight southern twang that he developed after years of listening to his southern grandparents speak. His calm demeanor had helped him learn how to ride horses as an eight-year-old in his uncle's driveway. It was also what helped him recover from falling off bucking horses when his older friends N-Dog, Rich-Rich, and Black first took him riding around the neighborhood. As the youngest one in the group back then, he understood from an early age that he learned more when he stayed quiet and observed.

★ ★ ★

The ranch was more than a place to ride horses. For nearly all the cowboys and other members of the community, the ranch was an ecosystem that gave everyone who stepped inside it meaning and a way to preserve their friendships. As twenty- and thirtysomething-year-olds, the years had passed and some of the ranch's elements had changed. The ten-foot-high basketball hoop that provided the backdrop for some of the most intense three-on-three games in Compton had been taken down, and the driveway was now home to a few older-model cars that had not been driven in years. Before everyone had horse dreams, each member of the cowboys, like others who grew up in Compton during the peak of the Los Angeles Lakers showtime days, had hoop dreams. But as everyone grew older and busier, the games slowly began to dwindle.

The difference between the world inside the ranch and the one outside was stark. Inside was a sanctuary where everyone came to find balance and peace. Hanging out could have easily gotten them arrested or fined had they been doing that outside on the porch. But inside the world of the ranch, there were different sets of rules. At the ranch, there was a protective barrier between their flesh and the hot pieces of metal that shot out of guns of the Nutty Bloccs, a local rival gang. Keenan and Layton had been chased back to the farms too many times to count, and each time they cleared it to the ranch, they knew they would survive. It was their safe haven.

Like the throwaway horses that filled the ranch, each member of the band was—at one point in their lives—also given up on at an early age. Black boys and girls like them were born into a world devoid of dreams, a world where the color of their skin served as a scathing reminder of difference and erasure. They were born into worlds that never gave blackness the chance to be cowboys and cowboys the chance to be black.

As time passed, these same children grew into full-fledged cowboys who developed inseparable bonds with their horses, opening spaces in their bodies for a love to remerge that the streets had once taken away. The horses listened when nobody else would and showed up when nobody else did. They cared for them unconditionally, and in return the horses taught them how to love.

Slowly, seasoned glares turned into smiles. And layers upon layers of pain and setback began to dissolve. The horses brought joy with them, and it took up permanent residence in their hearts. The horses, they witnessed, had the ability to turn the most aggressive gangster on the block into the sweetest, innocent version of who they were as small children. Kind. Quiet, even. Every horseback ride brought the cowboys closer to spreading this same feeling to members of their families, who continued to fight a war that almost always involved violence and addiction inside and outside their homes. Loving their horses helped them love themselves and those in their community, and though every horse was once heading to death, in the end the horses saved them, too.

The tradition of black urban cowboys came directly from the mythology created by the cowboys of the West. The telling of myths and legends was a way to endure long, cold nights on the prairies of the Great Plains or the frigid deserts of the Southwest. Cowboys lived rugged lives that fostered intimate connections with the horses they rode. Like the riders who once roamed the western frontier during the nineteenth century, the Compton Cowboys were also keen on survival tactics. The streets taught them how to escape danger and who not to trust.

But nothing was more important than the realization that they, too, had a better chance of surviving on their horses than they did on foot. The cowboys of the old West could escape dangerous situations at a moment's notice while galloping on their horses. Their animals had the ability to sense danger and could alert riders beforehand. At times the horses themselves became the armor during deadly shoot-outs or a barrier against harsh weather conditions.

Similarly, for the black cowboys of the Richland Farms, *not* riding your horse could mean the difference between life and death. In the old West, cowboys were fearful of bands of renegade outlaws and Native American tribes who fought tirelessly to protect their lands and traditions. The bandits the cowboys faced in Compton, in contrast, were warring neighborhood gangs and unlawful police.

A conversation between Keenan and Terrance took place in between their friends' chatter.

"Did your check clear?" Keenan asked Terrance. The cowboys had just done a photo shoot for a hat company, and everyone except for Keenan had gotten paid. It wasn't his first time having issues with his bank.

"It didn't clear again," Keenan said, answering his own question.

"It bounced?" Terrance asked. "What happened?"

"'Cause I'm black and I'm young and my hat's real low," Keenan said with a laugh, reciting a famous Jay-Z rap song. Terrance laughed so hard, he almost fell over.

"Chase Bank emailed me saying that the check had an irregular signature, but we called Chase and they said the money cleared but would be put on hold until the twenty-sixth. Man, this always happens to me. I need a new phone and I need to pay my rent."

When the basketball games gradually ended during their youth, some cowboys took up dirt bike riding, which at one point on the farms became as popular as riding horses. It was a phase for some, but not for Anthony and Terrance, who continued to ride bikes as adults in local riding groups on the weekends.

The music continued to play, and the group continued to celebrate Anthony's and T-man's birthdays.

"Help me with these cans, y'all," Anthony said while getting up to load the back of his truck with recycled bottles and cans that he had been collecting for months. The sound of bottles rattled as Anthony counted how much money he was going to make from this batch.

"That's ten, twenty, twenty-five, forty, sixty, eighty," he said, reciting the numbers. "Shoot, I may make me close to a hundred dollars on this run!"

"You better do the speed limit, man," Terrance said. "'Cause if you don't, the bums are gonna be happy if they spill out into the street, and if they find them, they'll definitely make it rain." He gestured a brushing motion over his right hand.

"That's at least a couple hundred right there," Rashid interjected in a deep baritone voice, looking at the collection of bottles that had collected in the back of his truck through a pair of dark sunglasses. "You got bottles, plastic, and glass. All the good stuff, man."

"I tried to teach y'all the game," Anthony said, smiling. "But y'all don't listen to me!"

Keenan and Rashid started roughhousing each other nearby.

"You better back up, you big-bad-wolf-lookin' dude," he told Rashid while puffing his chest out in the air. "I'm not a little kid no more."

"Oh, that's what you on?" Rashid asked.

Layton was back from the store with drinks and chips for Anthony and Terrance.

"Happy birthday, my guys," he said, passing the drinks and snacks around.

"Thanks, cuz," Terrance said.

Byron sat on a chair removed from the group. He listened to the conversations that the cowboys were having and reflected on his own life. The scene reminded Byron of the days and nights that he had spent with his own friends throughout Compton. The days when he didn't sell any CDs and was sometimes forced to steal from his own family to make ends meet. Those days were long gone, but the memories were crystal clear.

Two days had passed since Anthony's and Terrance's birthday, and Randy decided to call a group meeting on a Sunday afternoon. Everyone gathered around and sat on the bleachers in two rows. Charles, Layton, Keiara, and Terrance sat next to one another. The rest of the group sat on nearby chairs.

The energy of the meeting was solemn, and every word that came out of Randy's mouth felt calculated. It was a much different atmosphere than the birthday celebrations that had taken place only days before.

Meetings tended to be called only when Randy felt the need to address certain issues that the group was dealing with. Part of the increasing trouble he was facing was that he needed help running the cowboys and the ranch. The pressure was mounting, and with big plans for the future, including the renaming of the Jr. Posse as the Compton Jr. Equestrians, and the rollout of a ranch renovation project, it was time for him to acknowledge what many in the group had already sensed: he couldn't run the ranch on his own anymore.

Part of running the cowboys was establishing a code of conduct for everyone to follow. Like the gangs that operated around the ranch, the cowboys also operated on a strict code of respect and loyalty. Fights and internal conflict were mounting within the group, which affected the dynamics of the cowboys' relationships with each other and, according to Randy during the meeting, "needed to be out."

For instance, Keiara and Anthony had questions about upcoming photo shoots. Money was scarce for everyone, and some wondered how the selection process for shoots took place.

"Why wasn't I selected for that shoot?" Keiara sternly asked while holding her daughter Taylor in her arms. "What's your process like for picking who gets to do what?"

All eyes were on Randy while he took a moment to think

about how to respond. The young leader was trusted with the entire Compton Cowboys operation, and even though many of the cowboys were older than he was, they trusted him with a big part of their livelihood. Whenever a local company reached out to the cowboys to hire them for photo shoots, he was in charge of who would get selected. He was the mastermind behind the entire operation, and lately Kenneth had tended to be selected over everybody else, which raised questions among the group.

"It's a process that I have no control over," he said. "The people who contact me have an idea for who they want to see, and I don't have any control over who gets picked or who doesn't get picked. I wish I had more say, but I don't."

Everyone on the benches listened intently to what Randy had to say and nodded.

"Oh, okay, I see," Keiara said while Taylor squirmed in her arms.

It was the second meeting of the year, and Randy wanted to establish plans for the upcoming youth program. If the ranch were to survive, it would need to attract children. Each cowboy would have to volunteer and make time in their schedules to give back to the program, even if it meant less time for their own rides around the neighborhood. Then, toward the end of the meeting, Randy finally brought up the topic that everyone had been waiting to hear about.

"The ranch will continue to run after Mayisha retires," he

said as everyone's eyes widened with anticipation. "Anthony and Carlton will still have jobs, and there's nothing really to worry about. Everything will be fine. You have to trust me."

The news quelled some of Anthony's fears about the future, but it still didn't prevent him from thinking about other jobs that he could get should the ranch close down. He thought about his side hustle mechanic business that he had in the projects; maybe that could sustain him for a few months if the ranch closed.

At the end of the day, Randy believed, the only thing that could stop them was themselves.

"With that said, we have to do a better job at protecting the ranch," he explained while continuing to look into everyone's eyes. His voice softened, and he was on the verge of tears. "This is a real ranch and a real situation back here, so when we bring people here they have to feel what we feel. They have to feel peace, love, and harmony. Let's do a better job of handling our drama and all the behind-the-scenes stuff." He paused for a moment, scanning the group. He knew Mayisha's fears about the fate of the ranch. Money problems aside, the guys were going to have to become more responsible if they were going to keep the ranch alive. "We have to look in the mirror and ask how we each can contribute to the group and make the group better."

# SKITTLES

**LONG BEFORE ANTHONY LEARNED** to put a saddle on a horse, before he learned how to keep a Stetson hat crisp by brushing it counterclockwise, he was a gangster.

Anthony's initiation into the Acacia Blocc Crips occurred in the early hours of a humid late-spring morning on Acacia Boulevard in 1991. He was eight years old. His mother had recently walked out of the family, leaving his father to raise him single-handedly, a task that was nearly impossible for Thaddeus Harris, who worked as a high school janitor on the other side of town and couldn't be home to supervise or keep Anthony from being recruited into the local gang.

Anthony was alone in his house when three hard knocks

interrupted his breakfast and the voice of his older friend Tre boomed outside the double-bolted door.

"Come outside, Anthony!" Tre said. "Don't take all day."

He had spent the entire night thinking about this moment, knowing they would come for him at any time. He pushed his bowl of corn flakes aside, approached the door, rested his hand on the deadbolt, and peered out through the peephole.

Five people stood at the bottom of his front stoop. Tre, Marcus, and a few other kids from the neighborhood. They were between the ages of twelve and twenty-five, and each wore a blue handkerchief on their shoulder, a badge of honor that indicated they'd been inducted into the Acacia Blocc Crips years before. Like Anthony, they had all come from broken homes, but now they were fixed up as the youngest recruits who would be raised within the hierarchy of the Acacia Blocc Crips, one of the most notorious gangs in Compton. Feared by their enemies and by local law enforcement, the Acacia Blocc's operations centered on drug dealing, extortion, and murder.

Outside, Tre continued to yell loud enough for the neighbors to hear.

"Come on out! We know you're home."

Anthony unlocked the first bolt, then the second, and took a deep breath.

He thought about his family. Not the family of the dysfunctional home he was born into. Not the relatives his father had spoken about for years in his home state of Louisiana, or his mother's family, local Compton residents who had also journeyed from the deep South. The family that crossed his mind were the very people who would in a few minutes violently pound his eight-year-old body into the pavement in front of his house and all his neighbors.

The violence was justified, he felt. Getting jumped into the set was about proving your loyalty and earning respect. After this fight, he would have a family he could go to for anything both big and small, and they would always have his back. It would make up for the absence of love he felt at home.

In the city of Compton, these experiences were rites of passage, an intergenerational practice that began with Anthony's uncles and naturally carried over to him. If you lived on or around the Acacia block in Compton, you were either a part of the gang or you were against them. There was no middle ground. Those who refused to join would be tormented and harassed on a daily basis, and they were considered traitors and were often victims of violent assaults. The only people who received a pass were star athletes who showed promise on the field or on the court, and Anthony, unfortunately, could never dribble a ball or run routes on the football field. But he also wasn't a traitor.

Perhaps subconsciously, even then, a part of him recognized that he was born into an era shaped by forces outside his control. That he never really had a choice. That he would always—one day—become a gangster.

Outside, Tre wanted to know if Anthony was ready. He was one of the older cats in the 'hood and someone Anthony looked to for help his father could not provide. Anthony had shown promise—he was loyal and followed orders—and Tre finally felt like he was ready.

Anthony opened the door and stepped forward, ready to face the inevitable.

The fight that branded Anthony with the new nickname "Ant Dogg" lasted only five minutes, but it set Anthony on a treacherous path that wouldn't abate until fifteen years later, following a lifetime of gang violence, crime, and prison sentences.

Soon after the fight, when the bruises on his face and body healed, Anthony received his first gun from one of the gang's elders, a .380-caliber revolver. He kept it on his body at all times. He carried it on his walks to the corner store to buy soda and chips; he carried it to school on the days he decided to go. He and his gun were inseparable, particularly when the 7-0's, a rival gang, began a war with Acacia over drug territories. He even carried his gun to Martin Luther King, Jr. Community Hospital whenever he accompanied his grandmother for her checkups.

But he didn't fire it until two years later, when he was ten years old and the older gang members told him he needed to finally earn his stripes and forced him to come along on a drive-by shooting on a block controlled by the Tree Top Pirus, a local Blood gang.

He missed his target that night, but the gun made him feel invincible beyond measure. It gave him a sense of power that he never knew he could have.

The days came and went. Another test, another duty. A shooting, a drug run, a jumping. In a short time, Anthony was earning a name for himself for his valiant antics on the streets.

It was right after Anthony dropped out of middle school when Black told him about a woman he wanted him to meet. Her name was Mayisha, and she was teaching the kids in the neighborhood how to ride horses. Anthony had never been to the ranch before, but he was intrigued by rumors of horses and cowboys, of all places, right here in his city, his 'hood.

Memories of his father's recollection of his early childhood in Louisiana sprung back, images of the back-country roads he used to speak about, the grazing cows, and the rustic barns built on rolling green hills. Black had a feeling that Anthony would take a liking to riding, and he was right. Anthony was still a kid, after all, and despite the tough front he had to put up around the older guys on the block, he'd always been enthralled by the cowboys and horses he'd seen in western movies.

They set off for Richland Farms on a blazingly hot afternoon in August. When they arrived, they were hit by the pungent smell of hay and horse stables, and the whimsical and frequent neighs of the horses. Anthony had entered a world he never imagined. A world that he thought existed only on the lots of Hollywood studios. He couldn't believe what he was seeing. But this world was real.

They watched a group of horses trot before a row of swaying palm trees, and in the distance they saw the Compton City Hall building. It was captivating. Like an oasis in the middle of their city. It felt like a place he could call home.

Black pointed to a large sign above the entry of the stables. In bold text it read *Compton Jr. Posse: Equestrian Club, Est. 1988* and showed a gold painting of a horse rearing, as if it meant to throw off its rider. Anthony had never seen that word *equestrian* before, but a *posse* was like a gang, wasn't it? If so, he thought, then what did that make a cowboy?

He didn't have much time to figure it out, because a woman was already walking toward them. She was wearing a cowboy hat with a blue stripe wrapping its brim, and clutched beneath her arm was a dusty leather saddle. She had kind, sparkling eyes and a purposeful stride as she approached.

"You must be Anthony," she said, extending her free hand.

And that was how he met Mayisha Akbar and the Compton Jr. Posse.

★ ★ ★

Anthony was immediately drawn to the horses. He had never seen anything like them before; up until that point, the only cowboys he had ever seen were white. He quickly met other members of the posse, kids his own age with names like Rashid, Terrance, and Khafra.

Anthony, however, was leading a double life.

The time he spent on the ranch allowed him to unplug from the realities of Compton street life. The constant sound of the police helicopters that, he assumed, were chasing friends of his, continued to fly closely over the ranch, but while he fed the horses and cleaned their stalls, he was free. It felt like they were surveilling him, but he knew he was safe.

Being on the ranch opened him up to feelings of tranquility. When he was on a horse, he was exempt from his life of crime and violence on Acacia Street. But these moments had a daily expiration date on them.

As soon as he closed the gate behind him and stepped back onto Caldwell Street, he transformed back into Lil' Ant, one of the youngest and most ambitious members of the Acacia Blocc Crips.

"Alright, cuz!" he would yell to anyone he would see before leaving the property and heading home on his bicycle. "I'll see you on the other side!"

As a child, Anthony had always been attracted to flashy cars. He looked up to the ways the older guys on his block drove down the street in their blue chrome Buick Regals and Chevy Impalas as they listened to the sounds of Dr. Dre and their cars rattled from the powerful kick of eighteen-inch alpine speakers in their trunks. Anthony's love for cars also came from the time he spent with his father when he owned a mechanic shop on the westside of Compton. It was there where he learned everything from installing a speaker system to changing oil to installing a new carburetor.

His first car was a Nissan Altima that be bought from a friend for three hundred dollars. But it didn't live up to the emotions he felt when he saw a Buick Regal for the first time. It was love at first sight, and he would stop at nothing to one day own one.

He was faced with a choice: save up for a car the traditional way through working for his father, or make money the quicker route by hustling and drug peddling on his block. He chose the latter.

His first drug deal occurred on the corner of Acacia and Alondra Boulevard, when he sold a ten-dollar bag of weed to a local homeless man. His business immediately picked up, and within months Anthony had a consistent clientele.

Having money in his pocket felt good. It came quick, and every deal that he made came with an immediate adrenaline rush that he became addicted to. As the profits increased, the need to be in school every day dwindled. After getting kicked out of Compton High for fighting, he was sent to Inglewood

High School, where he was also expelled for fighting, and then ended up in a continuation high school, the last resort for at-risk teenagers.

While this was happening, Anthony also began to spend less time at the ranch. He had gotten a sweet taste for drug dealing and wanted more. After all, he still wanted to buy the car of his dreams. So he did what any young hustler in the 'hood would do: he moved on to selling larger and more dangerous drugs.

The coop was one of the most well-known crack houses on the farms, where Anthony began to spend most of his days. It was an ideal location, just close enough to Wilmington Boulevard, which was one of the main streets that surrounded the farms, but also quiet enough not to raise any suspicion. It was once home to a family but was repossessed during the early 1990s when they were unable to continue payments on their home and had since been used as a crack house by different dealers. The backyard once had a thriving chicken coop, but only the remains of wilted feathers and dried-up feces remained the first time Anthony stepped foot on the property. Every door—except for the back door—was bolted shut as a safety measure for both the inhabitants and the dealers who lived there. Every addict who walked to the front door was received either by Anthony or one of his trusted associates.

"What do you want?" he would yell from the other side of the door, while as many as fifteen people smoked crack cocaine on the living room floor behind him. Sometimes the drug fiends would stay for as long as two weeks, finding creative ways to support their addiction by completing tasks around the home like cleaning or delivering food for Anthony and his friends. Sometimes, when the fiends would get out of hand, Anthony would be forced to respond to situations with the threat of his gun or physical violence.

The money he earned at the coop helped Anthony purchase his dream car, a 1992 Buick Regal with one of the best hydraulic systems on his block. At seventeen years old, he was riding in style. His Regal came with a shiny navy-blue paint job, the same color of the bandana he wore on his forehead.

Earning money came with an even larger appetite for more. While he earned upward of five thousand dollars a day, he also supplemented his income by stealing cars. Sometimes he would get caught, sometimes he wouldn't. On days when business was slow at the coop, he and his friends would go looking for Mexican men to rob who wore expensive ostrich boots and flashy belt buckles on Friday and Saturday nights. Their boots alone would bring in at least two hundred dollars, and—if they were lucky—the men would have more money stashed inside them.

Anthony was eighteen the first time he went to jail for

grand theft auto. He had been caught a few months before he turned eighteen but released the same day because he was a minor. Being eighteen, however, came with a different reality. This time he was locked up for three weeks. A year later he was locked up again for possession of a firearm. A year after that he would be caught again.

An early August morning was the first and last time the police would ever bust into Anthony's home.

"Damn," Anthony said when he heard the door violently burst open. "They're here for me."

As his home filled up with more than ten police officers, he immediately thought about the movie scenes he had watched as a kid, films like *Scarface* and *Goodfellas*, which depicted the lives of Italian mobsters and illegal crime families. Getting busted, as each of these films depicted, was almost like a rite of passage. It was a way to earn stripes and respect, and when the officers busted into his room, he didn't put up a fight. Instead he calmly put his hands in the air, having known this day would eventually come.

As one officer handcuffed him and read him his rights amid the constant barking of police dogs, another group of officers reached under his bed and grabbed backpacks full of cocaine that he had hidden. A different group cut open his living room sofa and found other packages of cocaine. They had found his stash. But all Anthony could think about was the stash of tens of thousands of dollars that he had buried in his backyard. It was enough, he hoped, to eventually bail him out.

The judge didn't offer Anthony the bail he expected to receive, and his public defender, or public pretender as they were known in the 'hood, did as little for him as possible. He suggested Anthony take a two-year plea deal, which is exactly what he did. Within a few weeks he was off to a federal prison in California near the United States–Mexico border.

As a member of the Acacia Crips, he was relegated to a side of the prison for black inmates. As he settled into a cell with a black man from Northern California, he began to think about what his friends and family were doing back in his hometown. Being locked up meant that he would be forced to cope with isolation. While he sometimes ran into friends he knew from Compton, life in prison meant that he would be completely removed from the horses he dreamed about on Mayisha's ranch.

The first three weeks were the hardest and were unlike the time he had served in Los Angeles County jails, where his sentences had been a lot shorter. Being in a federal prison felt like an entirely different world, and he was forced to become tougher and more hardened the minute he arrived. He had to fight to let his fellow inmates know that he wasn't afraid of them. He had to man up quickly and find smart ways to survive within the prison walls. He did push-ups daily and fought other prisoners, often just to prove a point. If he didn't, it showed weakness in the prison and meant more difficult times ahead.

He got into a total of ten fights during his first three weeks, some with old enemies he had back in Los Angeles and others with inmates who were intent on testing him. Anthony got into so many fights that he got sent to "the hole" and sat in a room that was more isolating than his eight-by-six-foot cell. Solitary confinement was a dark, small, one-person cell that was created as a way to isolate testy inmates from the rest of the prison population. If the correctional officers believed you were in any way involved in a fight, you were sent there, the goal being to deter future transgressions. But the hole was also a way to break inmates down psychologically. It was a place where the screams and wails of grown men could be heard at night, echoing throughout the prison.

Anthony spent a total of two weeks in the hole's darkness. The only light that came into the room was through a small rectangular opening that he was fed food through three times a day. The darkness made it hard to see what he was eating, which he assumed was edible. It was the only time when Anthony would hear another human voice, even if it belonged to a white man who hated everything that the color of Anthony's skin represented.

"It's time to eat, Harris," the officer would yell three times a day, opening the window, then slamming it shut.

★ ★ ★

During his free time, Anthony spent hours exercising in the prison yard or running laps around the makeshift track that some of the inmates had created. He was never an athlete, but having a chiseled body and staying in peak shape in prison wasn't about impressing girls anymore, it was a matter of survival. The stronger he got, the better he could defend himself against other inmates.

Because he was a newcomer, he continued to make a name for himself by proving his toughness to the rest of the prison population. As a precaution, every inmate was housed in different cells and sections of the prison according to their race. African-Americans and Latinos, who comprised the majority of the prison population, were housed on opposite sides of the prison and had the largest sections of the prison. Race riots were common, and every section in prison was run like a complex organization, a Fortune 500 company even. Resources and money were allocated for different reasons according to one's needs. There was a formal code, and then there was the code that Anthony was forced to live by; some weeks were better than others. But Anthony wouldn't have to fight only his own battles in prison. He was often asked to fight on behalf of the elder and more respected inmates and to discipline others who didn't obey the rules.

As Anthony's first year began to round out, he found himself spending less and less time in the prison yard and more time in the solitude of his own cell. Though it had been years since he had last ridden a horse, in isolation his mind kept returning to the horses at Mayisha's ranch. Minutes turned into hours and hours turned into days as he dreamed about the feeling of riding bareback through the streets of Compton. He missed the feeling of working on the ranch and riding around the Richland Farms on Misty, the horse his father had purchased for him when he was eleven. When his cell gates opened up twice a day for recreation, he stayed inside and did push-ups inside his cell. He was slowly withdrawing from prison life and an environment meant to control him.

One day, he felt compelled to draw and paint, though he'd never done so before. He began to draw images of wild horses and aspects of the ranch that were vivid in his memory. He drew the contour of the giant oak tree that housed hundreds of chirping birds every morning. He drew groups of black boys and girls, as he remembered them, riding on horses wearing light blue T-shirts, like the ones Mayisha required everyone to wear on the ranch. Drawing materials were scarce, but Anthony managed to trade batteries for a notepad and pencils.

The first time he drew horses, they looked nothing like horses. The figures were weirdly shaped brown blotches that barely resembled an animal. But just like riding, practice made perfect, and after several months Anthony's drawings morphed into realistic illustrations of horses.

He began checking out books out from the prison library that had horses in them. He checked out children's books, history books, and animal books; anything that had images of horses that could serve as a model to improve his drawing. He spent hours sketching them onto another sheet of paper and putting them up in his cell, creating a makeshift horse art gallery for passersby to admire.

Inmates weren't allowed to have colored pencils or paint because correctional officers feared they could be used to make narcotics that could be sniffed or ingested, but Anthony worked with what he had and devised a method for creating watercolor painting in his cell using Skittles candy, which were a favorite among inmates and highly sought after. If the candy's color dye could leave a mark on his fingers, he thought, then they would be sure to also leave a mark on a sheet of paper. He was right. He dipped individual candies into a bowl of water one afternoon and shouted with excitement, almost shouting loud enough for the guards to burst in and shut his secret operation down.

Anthony learned that if he wanted to paint a brown horse, he would experiment by mixing red, blue, and yellow together. If he wanted a black horse, he would mix red and green Skittles. Anthony's drawings became lifelike with the color that the Skittles provided, giving them a texture that he could feel. He painted every day, sometimes long into the early hours of the morning while his cellmate groaned in the top bunk. Anthony crouched near the bars, painting under the dull, flickering light outside his cell.

In a matter of months, other inmates started calling him the "painter" and requested their own horse drawings.

The watercolor paintings that he painted every day were meant to keep him out of trouble. But they did more than that. They kept him alive. Drawing and painting horses for hours at a time helped him cope with the realities of being locked up in a cell meant to eradicate every ounce of humanity from his body. Being locked up took him away from his family and friends, and painting horses reminded him of the world that existed outside the eight-by-six cement walls and the humanity that every stroke of paint brought him closer to having again.

Every week on the phone, he spoke with Lozita, his girlfriend and the mother of his two children, and told her about his plans to ride horses and work on the ranch once he got out. She supported him and continued to send money to fill up his prison commissary so he could buy more materials for his paintings. During one call, he told her that if he had never stopped riding horses, he would never have gone to jail. She agreed.

As he painted more and more horses, he decided that this would be the last time he would ever spend time in prison. His daughter, Acacia, was five years old, and his son, Anthony Jr., was two years old. He wanted to be around for them and knew that getting back to the horses on the Richland Farms would be the only way to do that.

Two weeks after Anthony was released from prison, he decided he was ready to go back and visit the ranch. He felt the same nervousness that he felt the first time Black brought him there so many years ago. It had been more than ten years, and nothing had changed, he thought to himself. The blue-and-white *Compton Jr. Posse* sign still hung high over the ranch's entrance but was now weathered from past storms and in need of a fresh coat of paint. The storage shed that housed the hay, tools, and general equipment still looked like it was in need of a proper cleanup. There was more dirt in the arena and a few new horses, but everything else had practically remained the same.

Most importantly, he felt the same peace that he had felt as a child.

Anthony immediately spotted Mayisha sitting on the bleachers with a group of youth riders. Some were faces Anthony had recognized from the community, while others were new.

"Is that who I think it is?" Mayisha excitedly yelled as Anthony walked up to the group wearing a pair of dark blue jeans, an extra-large white T-shirt, and black Nike sneakers.

"You know it," replied Anthony as he approached Mayisha for a hug he had been dreaming about for the past two years.

As he and Mayisha hugged, Anthony looked at the tightly coiled dreadlocks that had grayed since he last saw her. Her soft blue-hazel eyes hadn't changed. Neither had her cinnamon light brown skin.

She looked at Anthony like a mother who hadn't seen her own child in years. As if her own son had just gotten out of prison for the same crimes she had fought so hard to keep her riders from committing.

Anthony, like the other riders who had ever been part of her program, would always be family.

"Welcome back, Anthony," Mayisha said as she held Anthony for what seemed like an eternity. It had been two and a half years since the last time they held each other. The warmth of her hug took him back to the memories of their camping trips and trail rides that she had organized for kids from the Compton Jr. Posse. Those trips, he remembered, were the only times he had ever left Compton.

She grabbed his arms and then his shoulders and looked at him with a pair of weathered eyes that had seen hundreds of boys and girls grow up from children to adults. The dark brown eyes that looked back at her were the same eyes that she had seen grow up, but something about them looked different. The brown eyes that she stared at had seen things in prison that no human should ever be forced to see: violence and terror.

Anthony wondered whether it would be the right time to

ask Mayisha if he could come back to work on the ranch as a groundskeeper. After all, this was the plan he and Lozita had discussed on their weekly phone calls over the past year. He figured that working on the ranch would be the only way to keep himself from going back to prison for a parole violation. He hadn't been an active member of the ranch since he was fifteen, and a lot had changed since then. He was an ex-convict and had very few options to find legal work. Most well-paying jobs required a high school diploma and would not hire an ex-felon regardless of their rehabilitation. The odds and the system were completely stacked against him, and he was faced with two options: go back to hustling on the streets or turn his life around by recommitting to horses and working on the ranch. His future lay in Mayisha's hands.

Anthony didn't muster the courage to ask about working for her that day. There were too many people around, and it would be another two weeks before he would eventually ask.

"You want to come back and work on the ranch?" Mayisha asked two weeks later. They were sitting on a bench overlooking the arena. Anthony nodded, a bottle of Sprite in his hands. "You know we don't have a lot of positions open right now, right?"

"Yeah, Mayisha," Anthony quickly replied. "I came to ask for a chance to work on the ranch. My parole officer said I have to find a job, and you know it's hard for people to find work once they get out of prison. If I don't find something, I'll go right back to the streets. Probably back to prison."

Mayisha looked out at the horses. "Maybe we can figure something out for you," she said. "There's already somebody working as the groundskeeper, but they'll be leaving soon. Come back next week and we'll figure something out."

Anthony was overjoyed. Drawing horses kept him alive in prison, and caring for them would help him stay alive back in the city of Compton. The old Anthony would have moved back to the Acacia block to be with his friends, but he knew if he wanted to stay out of trouble he had to live somewhere else.

Within a week he had moved into the Imperial Courts housing projects with Lozita and their children. His new two-bedroom apartment was humble but big enough for his family. Unlike his prison cell, his room had a door that he could open and close when he pleased, and a light switch that he could turn on and off.

The first few weeks were the toughest. Sometimes when he woke up in the morning, he would look around and pause, expecting to hear the barking orders from correctional officers who controlled every second of his life. It both relieved and scared him to know that the old order was gone, that the structure of prison life had become so ingrained in him that his body felt lost without it. When he couldn't sleep, he found himself waking up in the middle of night to check on his children who slept in the next room, like a protective father would.

The phone didn't stop ringing at Anthony's new home, and every time someone from his past called and asked for him, he would tell his daughter or his wife to say that he wasn't home. He knew his old crew would be getting in touch, and that meant trouble. On top of having to hide from his old friends, Anthony's new neighborhood also provided its own unique challenges.

The "blue bricks," as the Imperial Courts projects were called, were home to the PJ Watts Crips and close to the Grape Street Crips, who were located in a nearby housing project. Both gangs at one point had been at war with the Acacia Crips. As it stood, Anthony would be in danger, especially with a conspicuous *A* tattoo on the left side of his neck, which everyone in Compton and Watts knew meant that he was from the Acacia Crips.

To Anthony's surprise, nothing happened the first week he moved into his new neighborhood. He introduced himself to members of the PJ Watts Crips and assured them that he had left that life behind.

"I'm an old head," he described to the young men in the projects. "I done paid my dues already and lived that life."

After a few weeks, head nods turned into handshakes and then into hugs. People started calling him "OG Ant"—short for original gangster—as a form of respect. In the meantime,

Anthony and his family were busy catching up on the birthdays, football games, and holiday parties that they had missed while he was locked up.

Anthony's workday on the ranch usually began at five a.m. and ended around twelve p.m. His schedule allowed him to pick up his children from school every day in ways that he dreamed of when he was imprisoned. He never had been an early riser before, but he had grown accustomed to the five a.m. wake-up calls in prison. Being on the ranch before anyone arrived gave him a feeling of peace that he had desired for so many years. The early mornings were still and quiet and mysterious.

The more removed he became from the life he used to live, the closer he became with the horses on the ranch. Dakota, a ten-year-old black American quarter horse with short hair, became his best friend. He began to confide in her while brushing and braiding her hair every morning. He told her things that he couldn't say to anyone else and shared some of the horrors that he had witnessed in prison. When he spoke to her, his voice transformed into a soft, caring version of himself—parts of the boy who had left when he first got jumped into the Acacia Crips returned during these conversations. She listened. He spoke. It became a cycle that was repeated every single morning. He could be soft and tender and share anything with her, which combatted the message that the world had forced on him—that black men couldn't be soft.

The biggest thrill was the moment he freed her from her stall and let her run into the arena. It was a feeling he knew all too well. He related to her, knew what she felt. Freeing her from her stall every morning became the highlight of his day, as if he were atoning for all the days he was locked up. He knew what it felt liked to be caged up for hours at a time. Her stall was the same size as the cell that he used to spend his entire day in. His was surrounded by cement walls, hers was surrounded by long metal gates, and both were controlled by someone who decided whether they could leave. The resemblance was uncanny.

When Anthony rode his bike to the ranch every morning, he could hear Dakota neighing, waiting for him to open the gate so that she could jump and run around the arena and play in the dirt.

"I'm on my way, girl!" he would say as he walked to the back of the ranch.

Her joy meant everything to Anthony. The time he spent in prison had made it hard for him to express his feelings and fears. But he did not feel that around Dakota.

After a while Lozita also began to see this change. Anthony was opening up to her and his family in ways that seemed impossible before. He started calling his father more often. He smiled more and spent more time around the home.

When he picked up his children from school every day, he hugged and kissed them and told them how much he cared for them, how much he loved them. If they behaved well, he would ride to their school and pick them up on Dakota. This was also the point in his life when he attempted to reconcile the relationship he had with his mother, who had abandoned him and his father. Forgiving her for leaving him as a child was one of the toughest things he had to do. He did it with the help of Dakota.

On the ranch he became one of the most sought-out mentors. Children gravitated toward him because of his knowledge of horses and the willingness he had to help children become better riders.

"You guys know what the rules of the ranch are, right?" he would ask eager groups of children between the ages of eight and fifteen, the same way Mayisha had taught him years before. "Rule number one is you have to clean up the stables before you can ride the horses. Rule number two is you have to feed the horses, brush their coats, and clean their hooves. After that, and only after that, you can ride."

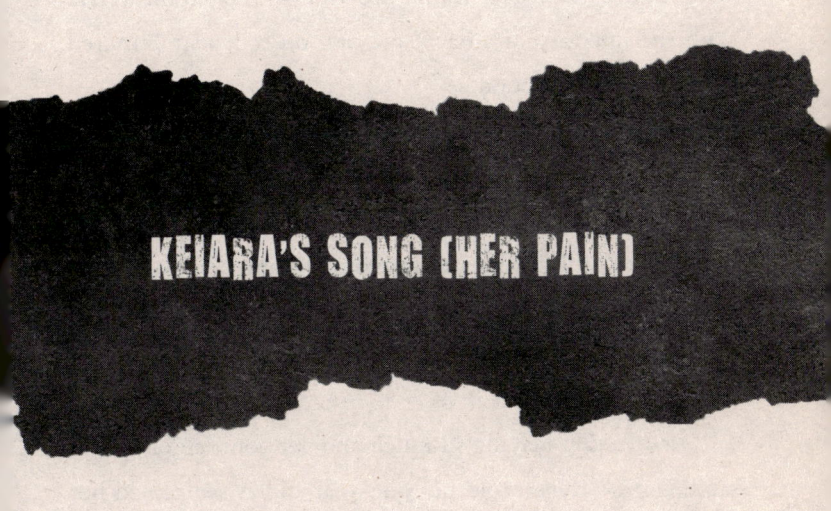

# KEIARA'S SONG (HER PAIN)

**KEIARA NEEDED TO CLEAR** her mind after the meeting, so she drove with Taylor to see a horse in a stable that was located in nearby Gardena. This stable had access to a larger riding arena and more room to ride and practice than the arena in Compton. Though she typically felt more comfortable around men than women, being the only woman in the group was becoming a growing challenge, especially when she and Randy didn't see eye to eye on things. When rides or events were planned, no other cowboy had to worry about providing childcare. Even those who had children usually relied on their wives or girlfriends. It was a luxury that she didn't have as a single mother, something the other cowboys didn't understand.

Taylor groaned and pleaded to ride Penny all by herself, without her mom. Her round brown eyes fixated on Keiara with the intensity of a hawk preying on rodents a hundred yards above the ground.

It's not that she minded Taylor's tantrum—she preferred it to complaining about not wanting to eat her vegetables every night at dinner—but Keiara could have done without some of her tears. Still, Taylor's enthusiasm brought her joy. Horseback riding had been in her family for three generations, and Taylor, she believed, would continue the family bloodline and keep the tradition alive.

"Taylor, stop playing so much and get your leg up in the saddle, girl," Keiara told her one-year-old as she placed her tiny body on the dark brown saddle while standing inside the riding arena. "Okay, you ready? Mommy is going to hold you, but you're going to be on your own, okay?"

Taylor nodded.

The breeze blew softly around them, gently moving in between Keiara and her daughter as she slowly pulled a brown mare, Penny, around the empty arena. Riding around the arena with her mother was Taylor's favorite pastime. When she wasn't riding horses with her, she was talking about riding horses. Her daycare teachers kept a tally about how many times during the day she spoke about horses; it was always a double-digit number.

She was a regular at the stables, and fellow riders all took a liking to Taylor, whose brown eyes beamed with joy around any horse she could get her hands on, big or small.

Being surrounded by horses was tradition for the pair. With deep roots in rural Mississippi, horses were a staple on both sides of Keiara's family for as far back as anyone could remember, beginning with Keiara's maternal grandmother, Mimi, whose husband, Spurgeon McClendon, bought her a horse when they arrived in Compton in the 1950s from Mississippi. Spurgeon introduced Keiara's mother, Jennifer, to horses, which she rode competitively until Keiara was a teenager.

Keiara walked the horse around the arena for about twenty minutes before Taylor started to get antsy. The glaring afternoon sun beat down, and her two pigtails bounced from side to side while Penny trotted slowly. After a few laps, Taylor's uneasiness picked up.

"Mommy," she softly whispered. "Mommy."

Keiara knew what was coming next. This was usually when Taylor's soft whimper would transform into a full cry, meaning it was time to go to the bathroom.

This time, however, her bathroom break happened to coincide with the break that Keiara also needed to give herself. Just a few days before, a sudden movement triggered a sensation in her lower back that swelled with a piercing pain that shot down through her entire lower torso. She rubbed the lower part of her back, right above the waist of her jeans.

Ever since she had a car accident the year before, her back had required months of rehabilitation and rest. It was her first major injury as an adult, and the most painful, because it forced her to take almost a year off from competing in the rodeo circuit. Not being able to ride and compete in the barrel races was one of the hardest things she had ever had to endure, because riding was all she had ever known. Even after giving birth to Taylor, she was back on the circuit in a matter of months. Nothing would keep her from saddling up.

Her entire identity had revolved around horses for as long as she could remember. They were central to who she was, and like Taylor, she had also begun riding when she was a toddler, eventually working up to competing in the Bill Pickett Rodeo, one of the only black rodeos in the United States, at the age of ten.

Getting healthy again was the number one priority for Keiara. Her dream of becoming the first black woman to compete in the National Finals Rodeo was no small feat given her work schedule and her duties as a mother.

On days that she didn't have to work, her mornings usually consisted of either a gym workout session or a visit to the physical therapist, who would perform hours of therapy on her back and her shoulder. Sometimes the sessions were painful, but they were the lesser of two evils: she preferred that pain to the agony of not being able to ride at all. On days when her daughter didn't have to go to daycare, she brought her along to the stables. Though she loved bringing Taylor along, being alone with her horse in the arena brought her the most joy. It reminded her of her first horse, a brown Thoroughbred named Skip, that she bought with her own money at the age of fifteen.

Like other children who grew up in Compton during the 1990s, her life was almost entirely consumed by gangs and violence. The violence usually occurred outside her home, but sometimes it also seeped inside. The home that she grew up in was divided by a front and a back house. Keiara stayed with her grandparents and siblings in the front, while her mother lived in the back, away from the family. Her Mississippi-born grandfather, the head of the family, was a stern man, and one of the only people in his family to migrate out west during the height of the Great Migration. He was the only father figure she ever knew, because her biological father was incarcerated when she was two years old and sent to a federal prison in Minnesota.

Like other black men who grew up in that era, her grandfather took to alcohol as a means to deal with the isolation and frustration created by the lack of opportunities that he found once he arrived in California.

The West Coast dream—that anyone could find steady work, that it was a place free of the entrenched racism of the

South—never quite reached fruition. He, too, found California to have its own system of racial inequality, often more challenging to confront because it wasn't on the surface. So he found refuge in the bottle. It also created deep tension in his home, often leading to verbal abuse toward his family.

Still, the violence inside Keiara's home was eclipsed only by what she experienced outside it. Bullets often flew from various directions in her community. Sometimes they flew out of the guns of black men who wore blue, sometimes they flew out of the guns of black men who wore red. Sometimes they flew out of the guns of the police, who wore black and white.

Though she was never in a gang, Keiara always had friends and relatives who were from the local neighborhood gang. Even if she tried, there was no way to fully escape the wrath of the 135 Bloods or the Westside Pirus. Growing up next to a group of horse stables called the hill, near the border of South Central and Compton, helped her escape the violence. She received a pass from the Pirus when she rode her horse around her neighborhood and became the "girl who rode horses" at school. Outside of class she was teased, but it never fazed her. It only motivated her to ride horses more often and to develop a language to communicate with them, a language of silent compassion.

At thirteen, she began competing in rodeos throughout the state. Her mother and her mother's friend would often be the only black people in attendance. She could remember being one of the only black people out of five hundred competitors, and nobody spoke to her until she started winning money. It was just her and her little black horse out there getting it.

With success, it became clear how unusual Keiara was. White competitors didn't want to see a black girl from Compton take all the winnings. It was her introduction to discrimination and to a world that labeled her a stereotype: a young black girl from the 'hood who had no business competing in rodeos. The reactions to her presence at mostly white rodeos made participating in the Bill Pickett Rodeo, a black rodeo circuit, feel closer to home. Being around black riders and competitors felt familiar, and she was instantly introduced to black riders from all over the United States, communities where black cowboys and cowgirls weren't the exception but the norm.

While Keiara competed in weekend rodeo events, an entirely different reality was quickly approaching. The brief stares and the glances she received from young boys and men evolved into longer pauses. She was beginning to receive attention from men in ways that she had never experienced before. Her body was developing, and by the age of twelve she was often taken to be much older than she really was.

At one point, she developed an innocent crush on her

best friend's older brother, a seventeen-year-old known for his good looks and popularity in the neighborhood. The hairs on her body rose whenever he entered the room, and she experienced new feelings for him that she feared sharing with her mother and close friends.

One night while sleeping over at her best friend's house, she was awakened by the creaking sound of the bedroom door while her friend slept across the room. The door opened slightly, revealing the contour of what appeared to be her crush, his broad shoulders outlined by the light of a moonlit window. He jumped into her bed and began to kiss and touch her, and when she wanted him to stop, he would not listen. At some point her friend woke up, saw what was happening, and yelled for him to get out of the room. Unfortunately, it would not be the last time Keiara would be pursued and molested by her friend's brother.

It happened twice, and both experiences haunted her and left her deeply confused about her own body. She began to feel that her body was not hers to own, that it was up for grabs. She feared telling anyone about the experiences because of the reaction that people might have. She felt ashamed, and the silence of the assault left her completely mute. The only friend she felt she could speak to about it was her horse, Starlight. Her emptiness hardened into resentment toward herself and others, and riding her horse became more than a hobby; it became a matter of survival.

Around this time she began driving, and she purchased her own vehicle to see her horse every day after school. At home, Keiara continued to hang out with local gangsters. She began dating some of them and often found herself in precarious situations, particularly after getting a *P* tattoo on the back of her neck with a crown and a star, an emblem that represented the Piru neighborhood that she was raised in.

Her family continued to be involved with different facets of dangerous street life. The life she led in school didn't always reflect the one she lived after school got out. She got into trouble at times on the streets, but she managed to keep her grades up while in school. She applied to different colleges and got accepted into Prairie View A&M, a historically black college located near Houston with a rodeo school. It was the only school that would allow her to continue to ride horses while attending. It was a dream come true and brought her closer to realizing her goal of becoming a national barrel race champion.

Still, leaving Compton was difficult. It was the community she had grown up in. But leaving her younger brother, Gerrod, was even harder.

Gerrod was well into high school by the time she had left for college. The two had grown extremely close as children; Keiara often felt more like his mother than his older sister. She had cooked and looked after him since she was ten. In high school, she picked him up from wherever he was at and dropped him off at friends' homes, ensuring that he was safe at all times. She even fought other boys in the neighborhood who picked on him because of his slight build. Gerrod meant the world to her.

Before she left, he had begun to mature right before her eyes. Though he was always affiliated with the local gangs in their neighborhood, he became fully integrated into the 'hood. He joined the 135 Westside Piru Blood gang right before she left for Texas for the first time.

"If you're going to join the gang," she advised him, "you have to lift weights and get stronger so other people won't overpower you."

While she worried about her brother's safety, being at a historically black college was transformative. She had never been around so many black people who prioritized education and also came from the 'hood. Her first day on campus, she met a young woman who had also attended her high school, and they became close and each other's support system.

But while Keiara was away, she also dealt with the realities of survivor's guilt. She questioned why she was the one lucky enough to leave the 'hood. She kept thinking about all the people she left behind in Compton and questioned why she deserved a better life than them, or rather, an escape from the violence that trapped them. Reconciling this reality made it hard to be away from her community, particularly as she noticed her brother sliding deeper and deeper into the streets.

Their phone calls became less frequent. Her mother called her and worried about Gerrod's safety. "I'm scared for him," she would say, and when she did speak with her brother on the phone, the conversations became superficial. There were things he was going through that they felt he shouldn't discuss over the phone. Code words were often used to describe the murders of friends and money that he was making from selling drugs. The roles had reversed. Gerrod was now the protector of the family and in control of the neighborhood.

Everything changed during the early morning of Sunday, September 28, 2014.

The phone rang at four a.m. Keiara was sleeping in her boyfriend's home in Louisiana, where she was visiting him for the weekend.

"Why is Kevin calling me this late?" she asked herself as she looked at her phone. Kevin was her cousin.

She ignored the call and fell back asleep. The phone rang again and again.

"Hello?" she said, still half-asleep.

"Kika, Gerrod's gone!" Kevin yelled on the phone while crying hysterically. "He's gone!"

"What do you mean he's gone?" she wearily replied.

Kevin's girlfriend grabbed the phone.

"Mimi just called us and we're on our way over to the hospital now," she said. "Call Mimi. Call Mimi."

After calling Mimi to confirm the news of her brother's death, Keiara broke down in a state of shock. Gerrod had been shot in the head by a member of the Westside Pirus in an apparent setup. They had been looking for him for weeks, and the streets had finally caught up to him.

She took a plane home the next day and cried during the entire flight. Coming home from Texas was usually a happy occasion. A close friend or relative would usually pick her up from the airport. But this time, the occasion was different. There was no celebration at their home, only the looks of people who had heard this song play before. Like Gerrod, Keiara's uncle had also died at the age of twenty-three. His death had left an open wound in her family, and now the wound had grown.

It usually took law enforcement weeks or months to find someone's killer. Sometimes it took longer. This time, however, the shooter took his own life with a shot to the head, using the same gun that left Gerrod fatally wounded on the sidewalk in front of Keiara's home.

After her brother's funeral, Keiara fell into a deep depression. The only consolation she received was the tattoo that she got in her honor of her brother's life, a Leo horoscope sign on her right forearm. She reverted back to the person she was after the molestation. She stopped attending school. She shut herself off emotionally from her friends and family and headed to the stables on a daily basis. Her horse, Skip, the same horse she had owned since she was fifteen, became a sounding board for her pain again.

It had been a year since she had last ridden, and the death of her brother was the inspiration she needed to begin training again for an upcoming rodeo. After working the horse early in the mornings, she would take it out on daily walks around the same neighborhood that she and her brother had grown up in. The walks became healing and therapeutic. Every walk was an opportunity to think about what she could have done differently. If only Gerrod would have committed his life to horses like she did, he would still be alive, she believed.

On the corner of Broadway and 134th Street, her horse's breath began to pick up and its knees began to wobble. He shook uncontrollably, forcing Keiara to jump off the saddle and into a horned bush. Moments later, Skip collapsed in the middle of the street. She placed her hand under its nose hoping to feel its breath, but nothing came out. While she yelled Skip's name, her horse's eyes suddenly began to roll into the back of his head, and within moments he lay in the street lifeless, a few blocks away from where her brother was killed just one month before.

The intersection of Broadway and 134th Street had historically been a popular murder location. It was just blocks away from Athens Park, home to the infamous Athens Park Bloods, one of the most notorious Blood gangs in Los Angeles. Dead black bodies on the street became the norm. A dead horse on the street, however, drew more attention.

After crawling back to her horse, Keiara took off her boots and began to weep in front of the crowd that had gathered next to her horse. She sat on the curb and thought about the death of her brother and her horse. Two of the most important things in her life had been taken from her.

While she was picking out her brother's grave lot only weeks before, two butterflies had flown onto her shoulder and remained perched there for several minutes. Butterflies had always been one of her favorite animals. They symbolized a fresh start and a sense of transformation following death or loss. Seeing both of them surprised her. Perhaps one of them represented her brother, she thought. As she sat on the curb looking at her dead horse, she realized that the second butterfly represented the death of Skip, her other best friend.

Time had healed some of the wounds that Keiara experienced as a child. Though she was back in the same neighborhood that had brought her pain, she was also back in the same place that brought her the most joy. Being away from Compton helped her understand that there was a world outside her neighborhood, and that she needed to heal from some of the wounds that she had experienced. As a twenty-nine-year-old single mother, Keiara believed that the amount of death she had experienced in her lifetime had prepared her for the past two years.

Her brother had been the one person in her life who continued to motivate her to ride and compete. Being the first black woman to win a national barrel racing competition would be the only way to honor his life.

A few days later, while digging through her closet, she stumbled on a barrel racing book. It was dusty and missing pages, but reading it was like a sign from God—it could help her become the champion she knew she'd once felt destined to be. So she turned the first page.

The death of her brother and her horse sent Keiara to a dark place. She had never really dealt with being molested when she was younger, and she was experiencing depression and insomnia. When her grandfather experienced frustration and anger, he turned to alcohol. Keiara's mother did the same. During the weekends Keiara followed this example, and for a brief moment it seemed to take away some of the pain, but it also brought her closer to the life she had always feared for herself. She knew she was moving toward a point of no return and needed to put an end to her behavior.

She decided to look for a therapist she could speak to about her alcohol addiction and ongoing depression. Making this decision was one of the most important moments in her life. It was the first time anyone in her family had sought out therapy. Her grandfather frowned upon it, and some of her friends wondered if she was losing her mind. But seeing a therapist and speaking about her brother's death a year after he was killed taught her more about herself than she had ever known. Every childhood trauma that she experienced made sense in the context of the turmoil she felt. She learned that the uncontrollable fits of rage that she experienced around people were a symptom of suppressed feelings. She learned about boundaries and began establishing them with her parents, who had been triggers in her life.

Still, she continued to wake up in the mornings and cry uncontrollably. Something was missing, and the potential answer to her problems had four legs. Her therapist helped her realize that horses had been her escape as a child, and reconnecting with them would be beneficial. Her new horse, Penny, could be the answer to her suffering, she thought.

Penny wasn't like the horses Keiara had previously owned. She was the color of a chestnut, stable and calm, and didn't buck when she tugged on his reins. With time and more practice, she believed, they could become a great team. Penny was more than just an opportunity for her to get back into the barrel racing circuit. The horse taught her how to be tender again. Horses don't respond to aggressive energy, so she checked her anger and confronted the reasons why she took her anger out on people. Penny softened her.

Penny also taught her about communication. Learning to be around an animal that doesn't speak forced her to tune into a part of her body that she had forgotten how to use since she was a teenager. She began to listen to her horse and, by extension, herself.

Within a year, Keiara was back on her horse and opening up to herself in ways that she never imagined. She started a women's group called Women Unity that met once a month at her cousin's home in North Long Beach to make sense of her pain and those around her. Many of the women in attendance were also single mothers, who for the first time in their lives spoke openly about anxiety and depression. The weekly meetings became healing circles that allowed her to share things that she had previously shared only with horses. She spoke openly about the sexual abuse, her temper and anger, and her mental health. It all began to make sense. Her angry flare-ups were rooted in the abusive environment that she grew up in, but also in the events that she had experienced in her life. The migraines that began in the fourth grade and that used to leave her incapacitated were a symptom of the stress she experienced at home.

Getting back to her training regimen was the most important thing for Keiara. As the only woman in the Compton Cowboys, it was her goal to help other black women become more involved in the sport. Barrel racing tended to be the only event offered for women at rodeos, while men could choose between team roping, calf roping, bull riding, steer wrestling, and bronco riding. Black rodeos, in particular, were smaller in scale but tended to offer women lady steer undecorating, an event that never interested Keiara.

Still, getting healthy would be her toughest challenge. Injuries continued to plague her recovery. In July, while she was driving through Compton, a car crashed into her bumper, immediately sending a sharp pain through her entire back. That night, when the adrenaline wore off, she fell into bed and had trouble standing. A visit to the doctor's office revealed that she had suffered four badly swollen vertebrae discs on her upper and lower back. *God had such an interesting way of testing,* she thought to herself while examining the X-rays with her doctor and hearing the news that she would have to be off her horse for at least another three months. Though her doctor had sternly advised her not to ride or do anything that might tamper with her recovery, she still had to care for her daughter, feed her horse, and look after her grandmother.

Keiara continued living through the pain, one day at a time.

# CLOSE CALL

**THE LATE-AFTERNOON TRAFFIC ZIPPED** past Keenan as he rode Sonny on the Wilmington Boulevard sidewalk while Kenneth and Carlton trailed closely behind on their horses.

Since moving to Inglewood with his wife and her daughter, Keenan had been spending less time on the ranch. His work schedule at his new catering job and his suspended license made it challenging to make time for the horses like he used to. Riding helped him deal with the pressures brought on by a sometimes sixty-hour work schedule.

Their horses' ears and tails were perked high above their heads, signaling slight danger as cars continued to speed only a few feet away from them.

"Remember the last time we were at Louisiana's and them

guys from Nutty was over there?" Kenneth asked while loosening Ebony's reins. He glanced over his left shoulder to make sure he was heard. "Remember when we sent those guys from Nutty that one time?"

"Yeah," Carlton responded while looking west in the direction of the Nutty Blocc territory. "What you think would have happened if we wasn't on the horses?"

"What you think would have happened?" Kenneth sarcastically responded. "We for damn sure wouldn't be riding here today."

The Nuttys had been at war with the Farm Dog Crips for decades, and in most situations, walking to Louisiana Fried Chicken would have been a death wish. But on top of the horses, the three childhood friends felt invincible, like real-life 'hood superheroes who were kept away from harm.

At this point in their lives, the horses were able to sense danger long before they could. The farm's horses had developed a sense for survival, and if the horses didn't feel safe, they would stop riding and sometimes turn around. While the horses guaranteed some safety, the past had presented an entirely different picture. Over the years, some members of the Nuttys had shot at riders from the farms who they suspected of being members of the Crips.

At the end of the day, nobody was really safe.

Sonny had been especially active during the entire ride. He sensed Keenan's own anxieties about riding so close to the

Nuttys' neighborhood and tensed up at every car that passed, both of them hoping it wasn't a member of the Nuttys. Part of Sonny's fears had to do with the abuse he experienced as a young colt, and the effects of a plastic toy gun that went off near his ear over ten years ago.

"These horses saved us," Carlton replied in a southern drawl as he rode with one hand on his rein while using the other to send a message on his phone. "They was trippin', but we got away 'cause we had the horses with us."

The afternoon wind began to pick up, making Keenan wish he had worn more than a basketball jersey, jeans, and blue Nike Air Jordan shoes to ride in. The afternoon traffic increased as commuters filled Wilmington Boulevard on their way home from work.

Louisiana Fried Chicken was a neighborhood favorite. It was only a ten-minute ride from the ranch and easy to get to using backstreets. If it wasn't Louisiana's, it was Mom's or Cliff's Burgers on Alondra Boulevard, where they didn't have to get down from their horses to order their food.

Keenan got off his horse, tied Sonny to a pole, and walked through the front doors of Louisiana's. A child with two braids in her hair eagerly looked through the window while Kenneth and Carlton waited outside, still mounted on their horses. The little girl looked at Kenneth and Carlton like she had never seen horseback riders with the same color skin as her. She pressed her face tightly against the inside of the glass and waved at the horses, hoping they would wave back.

Behind the heavily protected plexiglass, a Louisiana manager had other feelings about the horses.

"Who gonna clean up all that horse poop y'all leaving outside?" she brashly asked Keenan through the old speaker system. "I hope you don't think you just gonna come here, have your horse poop everywhere, and then ride way like nothing happened? You got me messed up!"

Keenan and the other customers inside the restaurant laughed. The only person who didn't laugh was the manager.

"You serious?" Keenan asked.

"Hell yeah, I am," the manager said.

"Alright, I'll pick it up on my way out."

"You better," she said.

After his order arrived, Keenan walked out of the restaurant and saw a pile of fresh green feces coming out of Sonny's rear end. It slowly piled onto another fresh pile that Sonny had left minutes before.

"You gotta be kidding me," Keenan slowly said to himself while still holding on to his bag of food. "Why you gotta do me like that, Sonny?"

He looked around for something to pick up the droppings but failed to find anything big enough to scoop it with. Horses produce almost fifty pounds of droppings a day, and in that moment, it felt like all fifty had just came out of Sonny's rear end.

"What you gonna do?" Kenneth asked Keenan while laughing and looking at the manager, who was now standing by the glass, gesturing her hands toward the droppings and using her arms to simulate a shoveling motion.

"I guess I gotta pick up this poop with my hands," he said.

A crowd of people gathered around Keenan as the face-off between the manager and the cowboys drew in other members from the community. Cars passed through the major intersection honking and yelling in support of the cowboys.

"Yeeeeeehaw!" someone yelled from a passing truck. "Yeeeeehaw!"

After a few minutes of internal deliberation, Keenan finally dug both of his hands into the droppings and carried them to a nearby trash can. Some people contorted their face in disgust, while others gathered around to laugh at the scene. It wasn't every day in Compton that you saw a grown man pick up horse shit with his hands.

"Put some of this in your combo meal!" Keenan told someone who laughed on their way out of the restaurant. "It'll give it a nice flavor."

Keenan brushed his hands off on his pants, saddled back up, and started riding in the direction of the ranch.

After a few minutes of riding, Sonny began to feel uneasy and continued to fight Keenan. At the same time, a red car pulled up near the group and honked his horn, startling Sonny and sending him into a panic. On the second honk, Sonny bolted south on Wilmington Boulevard, taking Keenan with him and leaving the rest of the group in the dust.

His gait continued to pick up speed as all four of his hooves floated off the ground for what seemed like seconds at a time.

Keenan attempted to regain control of Sonny by pulling hard on the reins and squeezing his legs around the horse, but he refused to stop.

"Sonny, come back!" Kenneth and Carlton yelled as Sonny continued galloping uncontrollably down Wilmington Boulevard.

The three friends and their horses were now sprinting through the streets like the cowboys of days past had done hundreds of years before. In the old West, their horses would have run to evade danger, but in this situation, it seemed like Sonny was running toward it. The sight of three young black men running full speed through the streets of Compton would have elicited different reactions from bystanders, who would have assumed they were running from the police or a rival gang.

Three black men on horses, however, almost felt like an optical illusion.

As Sonny continued to dash along the sidewalk, visions of Flower raced across Keenan's mind. Flashbacks of her dying body on the asphalt after she was hit by a truck haunted his every stride.

He yelled louder.

But his yells were drained out by the sound of Sonny's hooves. Part of Keenan felt like the uncontrollable nature of the moment was a metaphor for the life he had lived growing up: fast and daring and potentially fatal. It almost seemed poetic to die on a horse.

But while those images immediately jolted into his mind, images of his wife and her child—the daughter he had vowed to help raise—also consumed him.

Keenan was left with no choice. In a matter of seconds, Sonny would crash into the oncoming Wilmington traffic and take Keenan along with him. He could either brace himself for the collision, or he could jump off Sonny and try to guide him away from the cars.

*One . . . two . . . three*, he counted in his head before finally jumping.

He landed in between Sonny and the cars, acting as a protective barrier between the oncoming traffic, slapped Sonny's rear, and yelled into his ear.

"Why did you do that?!" he yelled. Carlton and Kenneth caught up to them. He panted and bent at his waist to catch his breath.

He continued to grab on to the saddle like his life depended on it.

"You could have died, Sonny!" he yelled. "You could have died!"

# GOOD KID

**"NEXT UP TO SPEAK** tonight is Randy Hook, a member of the Compton Cowboys," the council member said through a microphone. "You have three minutes to speak, sir." The city council chamber was filled with a variety of Compton residents. Some were there to speak, others were there to listen to the council's plans for the community.

In recent years the city of Compton had been under investigation for a series of corruption scandals, which broke the trust of the community, and local city officials were fighting hard to regain it. As a child, Randy had watched Mayisha speak at the council hearing on countless occasions. She had always been an advocate for more resources for the Richland

Farms, and her confidence boomed throughout the room, which made him proud to be her nephew.

As he approached the podium for the first time, he thought about the shoes that she had left for him to fill. He was the youngest speaker that night and had a vision for his community that was centered on developing more horse programs for Compton's youth. At one point in his life, Randy dreamed of entering politics—it was part of the reason why he chose to major in sociology in college. He adjusted his black Stetson cowboy hat and stroked his beard in front of the mostly middle-aged African-American and Latino residents. All eyes were on the lone cowboy in the room.

"Good evening, everyone," he said. "My name is Randy Hook, and I am a member of the Compton Cowboys. We're a group of horseback riders from the Richland Farms, and I'm here to speak about the need to put more resources into the farms. Horses are a big part of the community, and we think they could really help with the image of the city. As residents of the Richland Farms, we've been asking for more horseback-riding lanes on the streets, and we need to have cleaner trails by the canals."

Members of the council perched in their seats and listened to Randy. His cowboy hat, gold earrings, and nose ring alarmed some members. They adjusted their glasses and took down detailed notes. His speech captivated them, but entering the room while mounted on his horse would have created more of a splash, he thought.

He spoke about the power that horses continued to have on youth on the farms and the positive changes he had seen in them. But without the help of the city, the impact of horses would be minimal. Many of Compton's own residents weren't aware that the farms existed, and he wanted to change that. He wanted a designated trail throughout the city and signage that detailed the farm's geographic boundaries. There was also a need for new cleanup methods on the farms, for areas that had been neglected for too long and prevented horseback riding.

When his three-minute session ended, the city council vowed to allocate more resources to the farms and to schedule a cleanup effort over the next few weeks.

"Thank you for listening," Randy said.

For many of the council members, it was their first time interacting with the new generation of black cowboys from the farms. The idea of young black men on horses was a tough concept for some of them to fathom because most young black men Randy's age were either in prison or involved with gangs.

The meeting established him as the voice of the Compton Cowboys and of a neighborhood in Compton that sometimes wasn't even recognized by its own. Randy's decision to begin attending council meetings was spurred by recent conversations that he had begun with other members of the cowboys.

"We have to put the same energy on the community-building side of things as we do with the riding and entertainment side of things," he said to them in a group chat text. "What good does it do if we don't help our community?"

Finding ways to give back was an ongoing challenge for the group. Randy understood that the ranch had been established as a way to give back to the farms. As Mayisha's nephew, he understood that her dream had been to have a program that would put children's needs at the very center. Everything else was secondary.

At the same time, he also understood the challenges that came with that model. She had wealthy financial donors throughout the years, while the Compton Cowboys had none. The ranch was running low on resources, and the community of support that the Compton Jr. Posse had in the past was no longer a reality. For many of the cowboys, it felt like their own community didn't believe in their ability to run the ranch successfully. At times, it felt like they were being set up for failure.

The daily strains of running the ranch's operations were affecting Randy. Most of his time was spent on reestablishing the ranch's presence in the community. Every day was a struggle to secure meetings with potential sponsors and donors: the Los Angeles Chargers, the Professional Bull Riding Circuit, Dr. Dre—they were all on his list. If the ranch was to have a chance to survive, the cowboys would have to secure immediate funds to help jump-start the new five-pillar program that he wanted the ranch to be established on: education, business, athletics, guidance, and therapy.

Randy would have to learn a lot of these things on his own. All he could do was get up and try to be as productive as possible, not to waste a single hour. He was learning as he went along, even down to the basic steps—filing taxes, incorporating a company. Running a business and philanthropic group wasn't something he'd learned growing up. He was doing the best he could with the little he had.

Since moving back to the farms last year, Randy had struggled to find balance both in himself and in the community. He had left Compton to go to college and then moved to the San Fernando Valley to live with the mother of his child.

But being back home came with a rude awakening.

He began to feel the pressures of the streets in ways that he didn't understand as a teenager. He also began to see how much of an effect the ranch could have on the ability to heal an entire community. He felt the ranch had the power to save everyone. That despite the group acting like a dysfunctional family and the community's own challenges, it was all grounded in love, which they needed the ranch to nourish.

Being at the helm of the ranch meant that he had to confront personal challenges and find ways to rise above them. Mental illness had plagued his family for generations, including schizophrenia and bipolar disorder. He considered his own family dysfunctional, like a lot of black families in urban areas, and the mental health issues only made things harder. His aunt's suicide was the most extreme example, but he recognized a form of mental illness in everyone in his family. They had the same kind of emotional instability and anger problems he did, and yet none of them knew where it stemmed from.

As an adult, Randy had attempted to address his own mental health concerns by seeking therapy, but at this point in his life—with the responsibility of keeping the ranch afloat—his own therapy was put on the back burner.

When things began to pick up with the cowboys, Randy found it hard to sleep at night. Insomnia had been a frequent visitor throughout his life, but at twenty-eight and with the pressures of keeping the ranch alive, it had kicked into high gear.

As Randy drove through the city following the council meeting, the sounds of Kendrick Lamar's album *good kid, m.A.A.d city* played loudly. His full beard, gold earrings, and nose ring moved in unison while he bopped his head to the rhythm.

He drove through the city to find peace of mind, and he often found it in Kendrick's lyrics. He was brought to tears the first time he heard Kendrick's music in the driver's seat of his father's Toyota Camry. Keenan sat in the passenger seat, closed his eyes, and took in the Compton rapper's words in the same way. After listening to the song on repeat, they both sang the lyrics to "Sing About Me, I'm Dying of Thirst."

Both Randy and Keenan had grown up listening to rap groups like N.W.A but had never had someone speak to them the way Kendrick's music did. His music provided a soundtrack for their lives in ways that no other musician had before. Kendrick understood what it was like growing up in the 'hood, and many of the traumas and everyday struggles he experienced were Randy and Keenan's, too. Also, like Kendrick, they had grown up eating at Louis Burgers on Rosecrans, and both navigated through the same situations with girls that Kendrick often rapped about. They both also considered themselves good kids in a mad city.

Kendrick's music spoke to them in a way that the older generation of Compton rappers, like Eazy-E and Dr. Dre, could not. They were all dodging the same problems that came from growing up in the 'hood, and they were the same age and from the same generation. Kendrick inspired Randy to consider what kind of influence the ranch could have outside Compton. He hoped to create bridges between other black cowboys around the United States by adopting similar youth ranch programs in other cities. It could be the start of a movement. If horses could work in Compton, they might work in other neglected urban communities as well. There were black cowboys in Philly, black cowboys in Chicago, and new groups popping up in just about every American city. *It is making such an impact here*, he thought, *why not spread it elsewhere?* It could be the prototype for all other 'hoods in America.

There were more benefits to establishing horse communities than anyone even realized. The possibilities were limitless. So why not set up ranches in every 'hood and see what happened? He believed that the animals had a spiritual energy that was meant to be shared, and bonding with them gave new appreciation for the environment. At the very least, the horses brought smiles to everyone's faces—they lifted spirits.

The dream of uniting the Compton Cowboys with other black riding communities was both within reach and a challenge. Social media had allowed the cowboys to connect with other riders, and as each day passed, more and more black cowboys began to contact him about the need to create more programs for black youth riders. The incentive to create more riding programs had high stakes, particularly as the killings of unarmed black men by police officers continued to occur throughout the United States. Randy believed that the ranch could serve as a model to help decrease the violence. Black Lives Matter was about camaraderie and caring for other black people. These horses, Randy felt, could help save black lives, too.

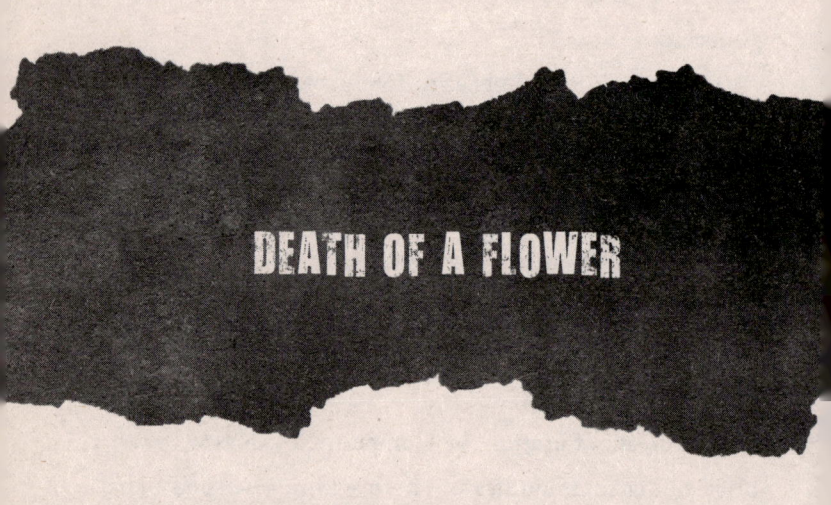

# DEATH OF A FLOWER

**FOURTEEN-YEAR-OLD KEENAN ABERCROMBIA** didn't mind when Carlton and Yaya, another teenager from the neighborhood, hogged his video games in his room. Playing Madden was a sacred tradition that few other things could match, and seeing both of them argue about the score was always a highlight. Carlton and Yaya had been playing video games in Keenan's bedroom for the past hour after getting home from summer school. The June sun was beginning to slowly set on Keenan's two-bedroom wooden home. It was a quiet afternoon.

"Touchdown, man!" Carlton yelled into Yaya's face. "You can't beat me!"

The banter between both friends continued every time one of them scored a touchdown. Sometimes one of them would do a celebration dance, which lasted minutes. They bet against each other, so money was on the line, but what they worried about the most was their pride. The winner would have bragging rights until the next time they played.

The afternoon light always found a way to seep in through the home's west-facing window, illuminating a series of horse paintings and figurines throughout the inside of the home. A photograph of an eight-year-old Keenan wearing a green Oakland A's baseball cap standing in front of his old East Oakland apartment building hung on the wall. Other photos of the Abercrombia family hung up on the walls next to it. A framed photo of Keenan's grandmother, a Creole woman from Louisiana, was by the front door. Another photograph of his sister the day she graduated from veterinary school also hung proudly near the front entrance. On the south wall were a pair of first-place medals that Keenan had earned at the Palos Verdes equestrian competition in middle school when he used to compete. Each served as a memento of a cherished memory.

Before Keenan and his mother moved to the home located between Mayisha's and Louie's, they had been living on couches throughout Los Angeles. Moving from Oakland had not gone as smoothly as Keenan's mother thought when they first arrived in Southern California. Rent was more than she could afford, and landlords required first and last month's rent at a time when supersizing a meal at McDonald's was a struggle for the young family. So they lived on couches with friends and relatives until someone they knew proposed the idea of moving into an affordable home on a horse ranch in Compton. For an animal lover like Keenan, that had sounded surreal. The lure of being able to live in a home and be around animals was an opportunity his mother could not pass up.

As a fourteen-year-old freshman at Verbum Dei High School, Keenan had plenty of summer school homework to finish. Mr. Katz had assigned an entire chapter of algebra problems that day, but variables and equations weren't more important than playing video games with his friends.

Carlton and Yaya continued to laugh and stomp on the brown carpet floor, worrying Keenan that they might wake up his mother, who slept during the day before working the graveyard shift at the airport.

"Guys, please keep your voices down, my mom's sleeping in the other room," he pleaded. "You remember how mad she got the last time we woke her up?"

His house phone rang loudly in the living room, but the sound of the video game and their conversations made it hard to hear. The fifth time it rang, Keenan heard it, jumped off his bed, and walked out of his room.

*Who could be calling right now?* he thought to himself. The creditors with the funny Midwestern accents usually called earlier in the morning, and the older women from church didn't call until around six p.m. Maybe it was his girlfriend, Tamra, who usually called during her fifteen-minute break at work.

Keenan picked up the phone and saw that he had four missed calls from Tre. For a member of the Farm Dog Crips, four missed phone calls meant that a close friend or relative was in a bind and in need of immediate help.

Or, worse, it could mean that someone had just gotten shot or killed.

"Keenan, it's me," Tre immediately said after a short delay. "Come to Oleander and Caldwell."

"What?" Keenan asked.

"Something just happened to your horse," Tre said in a soft and distant voice. "Hurry up."

"Flower?" Keenan asked. "What the heck happened to my horse? I left her in her stall, man," he shouted back at Tre, no longer concerned about his mother waking up.

Keenan's voice overpowered the video game, forcing Carlton and Yaya to pause it. They opened the door and watched him and waited, control sticks still in their hand.

"Man, I can't explain over the phone. Just come quick, man," Tre said before hanging up.

Keenan put the phone back on the receiver and threw on a pair of blue Nike low-top cross-trainers and bolted out of his front door, still wearing the same white tank top and basketball shorts he had slept in. He slammed the iron security door behind him, rattling the entire home, and blindly sprinted toward Oleander Street without knowing what awaited him, and never pausing to survey the street for enemies.

All he could think about was Flower as he sprinted past Mayisha's house, past Mr. William's home, and past Robert F. Kennedy Elementary School, toward the intersection of Caldwell and Oleander Street. The falling sun beat the back of his neck while he continued to sprint. Drops of perspiration began to build up on his body as each arm swing and stride pumped adrenaline through his veins.

When he finally got to Oleander, he was met by a police officer who redirected traffic away from the middle of the street. A large crowd of people gathered behind the officer, but Flower was nowhere to be found, only geometric shapes outlined by white chalk on the black asphalt. A few yards away, two pieces of what looked like a car bumper were circled by the same white chalk. Nearby, another piece of a car bumper was circled with the same white chalk.

As he approached the scene, another officer was busy unfolding a large white body bag from the trunk of his car. Still no sign of Flower.

He finally pushed through the crowd of black and brown people to see everyone's eyes were focused on a large mass on the ground.

It was a familiar scene that had played out in the community many times before. Only this time it wasn't a human body; it was his best friend and horse, Flower, a reddish-brown Arabian mix with white stripes and a white star on the ridge of her nose.

Flower's body quivered on the hard ground as she gasped for air. It had been nearly thirty minutes since she had gotten hit by an SUV truck in an apparent hit-and-run accident. The sound of her breath and pulsing of her heart suggested that she was minutes away from closing her eyes for the last time.

In Keenan's presence, Flower had always felt a sense of calm, mitigating the abuse she had experienced before she arrived at the farms. But even Keenan's soothing demeanor could not quell the pain and fear that ran through her body now. She looked at Keenan with the same eyes reserved for someone who has betrayed your love.

Keenan refused to make eye contact. He felt guilt and shame. Worse, he felt like he had failed on the promise he had made to protect her when he bought her for a hundred dollars at a horse auction.

Behind him, a few bystanders explained how a midsized SUV truck had been recklessly speeding through the farms before its front bumper violently collided with Flower's right leg. The horse had been clipped while the car was driving at more than fifty miles per hour, severing her leg and sending it twenty feet away from the rest of her body. Eyewitnesses remembered hearing the truck hit the brakes, followed by a loud thud that could be heard from blocks away.

"The truck just hit the horse and drove off," one person said. "We heard a loud boom."

Flower's exposed limb bled profusely next to Keenan, forming two dark puddles. Her ligaments and muscles erratically convulsed following every breath that she took. Somebody told Keenan that Chuck, an older horseback rider from the neighborhood, had taken Flower out for a walk without Keenan's permission. He came back minutes after Keenan arrived, attempting to explain what had happened.

"I'm sorry, man," he repeated three more times. "I'm sorry, man . . . I'm sorry, I'm so sorry."

Keenan didn't want to hear it.

Chuck had broken one of the most important codes on the farms: you do not ride someone else's horse without their owner's permission. His repeated attempts to console Keenan and amend the situation by offering him two hundred and fifty dollars only made Keenan more furious.

"You think that's going to bring my horse back to life? Two hundred and fifty dollars!" he yelled in Chuck's face. "What the hell is wrong with you?!"

He turned away and knelt down to rub Flower's long jawline. Tre made his way through the crowd of people accompanied by Keenan's mother, and both put their arms around him in an effort to console him.

"It was never supposed to end this way," Keenan said, drying his tears with the reverse side of his T-shirt. "Flower didn't deserve this. Why did she have to die the same way homies die? A drive-by."

"It's all messed up," Tre said, and put his hand on Keenan's shoulder again.

Despite continuing to rub Flower's jaw, Keenan still refused to make eye contact with the dying animal.

One of the officers approached him. He was white, young, and burly, with a shaved head. "What do you want to do with your horse?" the officer asked.

Keenan silently stood up and looked at the officer.

"You have two choices," the officer continued. "We can either put her down now or you can pay to get her transported to a hospital. It's your call."

Keenan would later learn that the officer was a rookie on the police force and had the disposition of someone who was eager to use his firearm for the first time since firing it at the police academy. The officer hadn't seen much action on the force since he had joined over a year ago, so it was thought he might have been eager to finally use the shotgun that he carried in his squad car.

Keenan ignored the officer's request and knelt down to rub Flower's coat again. Death always seemed to find a way to sit next to him. He was used to seeing men dying on the streets, but holding his horse as she gasped her last breaths brought him closer to death in a way that he had never experienced before.

"What you wanna do?" Tre asked Keenan, staring at the puddle of blood that had now formed around his white sneakers.

Keenan and his mother were already struggling to make rent every month, much less pay for the cost of moving Flower to an animal hospital to replace her leg. On top of that, bill collectors called their home every day threatening to damage their credit by moving their past-due bills to private collection agencies.

He had to make the toughest decision of his life.

After minutes of deliberating, Keenan responded to the officer with a silent nod, prompting his mother to walk back to her car to look for a pair of scissors. In the horse community, cutting a horse's tail before its death was considered a sacred act. It was believed that an owner could preserve the memory of its soul by keeping its tail.

She returned moments later with a pair of scissors and cut the brown tail, handing it to Keenan, who turned around and immediately began walking home, refusing to see Flower's death.

Before Keenan made a right on Caldwell Street, two blasts from the officer's twelve-gauge shotgun rang loudly behind him, echoing shock waves that could be heard throughout the farms. His legs gave out and he dropped to the pavement, sobbing uncontrollably.

★ ★ ★

The death of Flower would permanently change Keenan. After her death, he had nothing left to live for. She was his best friend and had been taken from him the same way the streets tended to settle scores: through death or violence. Seeing her lifeless body on the street, her eyes searching for his, gave him permanent nightmares and affected his sleep for months. He'd often wake in the middle of the night, crying out her name, still seeing the dark blood on the pavement.

He wanted revenge, but he didn't know where to find it. He stopped riding horses. He gave up being a cowboy. The death of Flower put him on a path of destruction that led to robberies, shoot-outs, drug use, and violence toward anyone who stood in his way. Within months, he dropped out of high school and began spending less time on the ranch and more time with members of the Farm Dog Crips. He began to put in more work and earned his stripes, committing a number of violent crimes against enemy gangs with the hope of gaining respect from the older members of the gang. Keenan found family and acceptance in the other boys and men who were part of his gang, replacing the companionship he lost with Flower's death.

It would not be until many years later that he found the courage to return to the ranch and, through his love of horses, save himself and get back on the right track.

# FLYING BACK

**AS THE PLANE BEGAN** its descent toward Los Angeles, Charles looked over the passenger next to him to see the city's bright lights.

Keiara was sound asleep in a different aisle, still wearing the travel neck pillow that she had been wearing since they both took off from the Denver International Airport after spending a week in Colorado at a horsemanship conference. He marveled at how calm she looked while the plane flew thousands of feet in the air.

It was only the second flight that he had ever taken, and he hoped for a safe landing through it all. Every bit of turbulence made him put his head in between his legs followed by a lengthy prayer.

"Lord, please don't let me go out like this. Lord, don't let this be the time and place," he said. When the turbulence settled, he looked out of the window again.

Every yellow light that flickered kindled his curiosity. He wondered which one of the lights belonged to his family and friends and which belonged to the home where his children were sleeping.

He took a deep breath and moved back further into his seat.

The city looked so much larger than it did from the streets of Compton. It seemed infinite and vaster than he had ever imagined. The concerns that he had about the future and the welfare of his children seemed minimal compared to the size of the city. His mind was clear after spending a week in Colorado as an invitee to the Patagonia horse summit; it was an honor, and something he had never imagined he would be invited to as a teenager.

But being around nature and in the presence of strangers made him appreciate the people he knew back in his city. He thought about reaching out to Tre. Maybe it was time to step up and admit some of the responsibility for their fight earlier in the year. It also made him reflect deeply on his reasons for riding and not riding.

It had been almost six months since Charles had last ridden or jumped. Part of the separation was due to scathing pain that he felt every time he tacked his horse to ride. At this point, his dream of becoming an Olympian festered deep in his heart like an open, untreated wound. It burned every time he was around horses. Perhaps his dream to compete in the Olympics was over the minute Susan had called to tell him that she could not train him anymore. But not trying would be going against everything he had been teaching his children, he thought.

He knew he couldn't give up.

The morning after flying back from Colorado, Keiara sat for a moment in her bed. In only a few minutes Taylor would come storming into her bedroom to wreak havoc. This was the only tranquil moment she'd experience for the rest of her day.

"Dear God, thank you for blessing me with another day," she said while closing her eyes and placing both hands on her knees. "Please look after my safety today and look after the well-being of Taylor. Thank you for helping me through this time, and please continue to help my back heal."

Before her back injury, her morning prayers were geared toward her own well-being and Taylor's, but the recent re-injury had forced her to revise her prayer. She was going to need all the help she could get after the doctor told her she would have to take a four-month hiatus from riding. Religion had never been a big part of Keiara's life before her twenties, but at twenty-nine, it had become as central a force in her life as horses were.

She was surprised Taylor hadn't barged in yet, as she did most mornings. "Taylor!" Keiara yelled, now finished with her prayer. "You hungry?"

Taylor walked into her bedroom and looked at her mother with quiet eyes. It was the face she made when she was undecided about what to eat. "Eggs it is," Keiara said to herself as she stepped over one of Taylor's toys on her way to the kitchen.

Living alone with Taylor was something Keiara had never imagined. As a teenager, she had always been drawn to children, and it was one of her dreams to have a home and a big family. When she started dating Taylor's father, they had spoken about having children. But when she approached him with the news that she was pregnant, he immediately stopped answering her phone calls and seeing her. After repeated attempts to reconcile their relationship, she decided to stop trying to contact him. Being a single mother was something she never envisioned doing, but with the help of her friends and family, it couldn't be that hard, she figured.

Part of her was also grateful that her brother had been killed before she met Taylor's father. Gerrod wouldn't have let her baby's father get away with what he did, and he would have paid the price with his life for abandoning her.

As she cooked Taylor a batch of scrambled eggs, she thought about the times she had cooked for her brother as well. She first started cooking and taking care of him when she was only ten years old. Sometimes it felt like she was his mother and not his older sister.

Every time she bent her back to reach into the refrigerator or moved the silicone spatula inside the pan, another sharp pain shot down her back. "Ouch," she said while rubbing the sore spot. "I just want this pain to go away already."

As a daily caretaker for an elderly patient, Keiara had a flexible schedule that allowed her to take Taylor to daycare at ten a.m. and complete other tasks throughout the day, like caring for Mimi, her elderly grandmother, feeding her horse, and keeping up with her weekly two-hour physical therapy appointments.

When winter arrived later that year, her back was nearly 80 percent healed, and doctors hoped that she would be able to compete again starting in March. Her gym workouts increased along with her physical therapy. The winter months had a way of keeping rodeo riders indoors, but for Keiara, winter was when she began to get back to her old self.

The next few months would also be the time to make a decision. Working as a caretaker and occasionally riding wasn't going to help her get any closer to achieving her professional barrel racing dreams. She looked at Taylor while her baby girl ate cereal and watched morning cartoons, wondering if she could ever provide a stable environment to raise her daughter and achieve her dream.

# MAXED OUT

**"GET OUT OF THE WAY**, Zoe!" Kenneth yelled at the top of his lungs. He was sitting on his horse, Ebony.

Zoe was his long-snouted, black-and-brown-haired German shepherd. She had been barking at Ebony for the past ten minutes in front of the green gate that separated his home from the street. Kenneth's morning had already started on the wrong foot, and Zoe was only makings thing worse. Usually by this time, minutes before noon, Kenneth would have already ridden around the neighborhood a few times.

"Zoe!" he yelled, loud enough for the neighbors to hear while simulating a throwing motion with his right arm.

The two-year-old German shepherd jumped back and

retreated toward the rosebushes that lined the gravel driveway, creating enough room for a smooth exit. Kenneth loosened the reins and gave Ebony a kick on her sides.

"Come on, Ebony, let's go!" he yelled, then at Zoe as he passed her, "Next time, I'm going to let her kick you!" Ebony began to pick up speed, her horseshoes thudding hard on the empty paved street ahead.

Kenneth and his mother first stumbled on the ranch by mistake. When he was in middle school, a friend of Kenneth's recommended a horse ranch in Compton as a way for him to be around other black riders.

"There's a ranch in Compton called the hill where you ride horses with other black people," his friend Victoria said to him one day at school.

His mother, Susan, worried when he complained about the lack of black riders at his competitions. As a twelve-year-old, his equestrian experience had been entirely white and he felt uncomfortable being the only black rider at events. The idea of having Kenneth around other black riders excited the Atkins family; they believed it would help him develop friendships with other African-American riders his age.

Finding the ranch, however, was one of the biggest challenges. They were given only the cross streets for the horse ranch. "You can find the ranch on 131st and Figueroa," Victoria explained to Kenneth's mother.

While driving to the ranch one day, they accidently got

off on the wrong exit and ended up on the south side of Compton, which resulted in an hourlong search, to no avail. The family returned home. A week later, a Google search with the keywords "black horse ranch Compton" brought the Compton Jr. Posse to the top of the search bar.

It would be the ranch on Caldwell Street. Susan and Kenneth made plans to meet up with Mayisha and get the grand tour of the ranch. Shortly after, the Atkins family decided to purchase property in a home adjacent to the ranch, so sure were they that it needed to be a part of their daily life. It was a large enough property to own horses and build a home for their son to be around other black horseback riders.

Ebony was one of the few Tennessee walking horses on the farms and one of its fastest. She belonged to a breed of horses that were first introduced on farms in the southern United States and that were known for their unique four-beat walking patterns. Their speed and elegance made them prized possessions in the horse-riding community.

While they rode, Kenneth's chiseled, tattooed brown body shined brightly as the Compton sun hit the top of his head, casting even shadows on both sides. The tattoos that covered the entire top half of his shirtless body each had a different story to tell. His first tattoo, the initials of his first and last name on the back of his forearms, was done the day after he turned eighteen. A cross with clouds on his right shoulder came next, followed by the word *rebel* on the inside of his left arm. On the outside of his left arm, in bright red, was the image of a fully detailed Lamborghini being pursued by a police helicopter.

While each of his tattoos was important to him, two stood out from the rest. His bold-inked Los Angeles tattoo with a city skyline background on the top of his stomach was the most visible and the most recognizable. The other was a hand-drawn set of three horses, two of which represented Ebony, the other of which was a tribute to the famous French general Napoleon Bonaparte, one of his childhood heroes because of his short stature and military prowess.

Many of the cowboys already disliked Kenneth for the way he treated his mother and his cocky attitude. They also disliked the lifestyle he lived, regularly bragging about his riches and fame on social media.

Tichenor street was empty except for a few cars that were parked next to the wooden logs that separated the street from the horse path. Most of Kenneth's neighbors worked during the day and came home around the same time every evening. That meant it was usually just Kenneth and Ebony riding around the farms.

A few men gathered outside their home to watch Kenneth and Ebony as they rode in the direction of the convenience store. One of them waved, while others stopped to take photos of Kenneth. The sight of a black man on a horse riding bareback through the farms still caused deep fascination among many of the newly arrived Mexican residents.

"Hey, black cowboy!" an elderly Latino man said in a strong accent. He was driving a van full of people next to Kenneth. "Alriiiiight," he said while driving away, gesturing a thumbs-up. The children in the backseat waved and recorded him on their phones as the van sped away.

Kenneth never minded the extra attention he received when he rode around the farms without a T-shirt. Riding shirtless and without a saddle was, to him, the ultimate sign of rebellion. It fed into his bad boy image and, he believed, helped him with the ladies. "Every woman likes a shirtless cowboy," he said to the guys.

Riding Ebony through the farms also reminded him of the cowboy westerns he used to watch with his older brother as a child. Even though the white cowboys tended to be depicted as the good guys, he had always rooted for the Native Americans since the day his mother first mentioned that he had Cherokee blood on both sides of his family tree.

Kenneth pulled Ebony's reins to the right once they hit Center Street, next to a Spanish-style home with a large green cactus that stretched onto the street. He'd mastered the ability to ride and text simultaneously on his phone while listening to music on his headphones, bobbing his dreads to the lyrics of Young Dolph, his favorite rapper.

★ ★ ★

Ebony was Kenneth's only form of transportation. Without a car, Kenneth rode Ebony wherever he went, which brought them closer together and gave his mother some peace, knowing that her son wouldn't be driving on the streets.

Kenneth had recently had conflicts with KJ, Mayisha's grandchild, who had just moved back to the ranch from Arizona. Their problems stemmed from a transaction involving Eugene, the youngest member of the cowboys, who was interested in purchasing KJ's mini motorcycle. Kenneth got wind of the price and accused KJ of trying to take advantage of the younger Eugene. A day later, KJ got into an argument with Carlton, his first cousin, and punched him in the eye, fracturing his eye socket. Kenneth rode over to KJ's home the next day and confronted him.

Each altercation that followed began to involve more members of the Hook family, including KJ's father, Khafra; Randy; and Louie. A rift between the Hook family was emerging, and Kenneth was caught in the middle of it.

As Kenneth rode Ebony west on Tichenor toward Center Street, he thought about the throbbing that had now spread toward the back of his head. Just that morning, he had another fight with KJ. This time, KJ's father, Khafra, was involved. As Kenneth and KJ fought in the front of their home, KJ's sister ran behind Kenneth and pulled two braids from his hair, tossing them into the air while KJ pounded Kenneth's face with his fists.

The fight lasted for a few minutes before Anthony and Keenan, who had been working in the back of the ranch, heard the commotion and sprinted to the front to break up the fight. A crowd from the neighborhood had gathered around them, leaving Ebony out of plain view. While they fought, she trotted away, only furthering the confusion Kenneth felt when he finally regained his senses and couldn't spot her.

"I told him he didn't want none of me!" KJ yelled out as his sister and his father grabbed him from atop Kenneth's body as he yanked some of his dreads out of his hair.

"I'm gonna max him out again if he ever comes back," he continued to yell to a growing group of people who had gathered outside his home. Although KJ was a teenager, he had the body of someone well into his twenties. He was stocky, and the veins in his muscles raged with anger.

"Kenneth, get out of here!" Anthony yelled while shoving him in the opposite direction. "What is wrong with you? Get out of here."

"Where is my horse?" Kenneth finally asked while picking up what was left of his dreads on the ground. "Where did Ebony go?"

"She ran that way," Anthony said, pointing in the direction of Wilmington Boulevard. "Go!"

A disoriented Kenneth ran to fetch Ebony with a series of new bruises on his head and less hair than he had woken with up that morning.

Something about this fight felt different from the rest of the altercations that Kenneth had had with KJ. The fight seemed like a breaking point for the rest of the guys, particularly for Anthony, who had warned Kenneth not to go back to KJ's house ever again.

Anthony's patience was running low, and his own feelings for Kenneth were changing. On top of that, there were other differences that he had with the rest of the cowboys.

Kenneth was the son of hardworking parents who had acquired middle-class wealth and stability and had given him everything he wanted as a child. They owned homes in Ladera Heights, an African-American middle-class community in Los Angeles, and owned the property located behind the ranch. Everyone on the ranch believed that his parents enabled Kenneth's antics by providing a rent-free home for him to live in and a weekly allowance. Kenneth never had to hustle for what he wanted, much less commit crimes like most members of the cowboys had been forced to do throughout their lives, and he was often resented for it.

"I'm done with him, man," Anthony told Keenan and Layton, who had just arrived. "He needs to be out of the group."

"He has to go," Keenan replied.

"Yeah, he do," Layton said, nodding.

It wasn't the first time that Kenneth would be kicked out or suspended from the group. Randy was aware of Kenneth's bad behavior, but he was also living in a spare room in Kenneth's home. After living in his car, Randy decided to move in with Kenneth and struggled to confront his new roommate. But the balance between acting as the cowboy's manager and Kenneth's roommate wasn't easy. His reluctance to ban him from the group's activities was not only furthering the gulf between Kenneth and the group, it was also raising questions about Randy's leadership. Kenneth had been suspended from the group on countless occasions, but now members wanted him to seek help for his alcohol problems and other issues or face permanent removal. They were on the edge, and something had to change quick.

Everyone's patience was running out.

Kenneth knew that his behavior was affecting the group's morale. He knew everyone was disappointed in him, and if he drank, his behavior was even worse. On his good days, he was just Kenneth—a loving, goofy, and joyful person to be around. He was the person everyone had fallen in love with when his parents first bought the home behind the ranch when he was eleven. But if he drank, he transformed into someone entirely different. He turned into Stona mane, his alter ego, a cantankerous version of himself that the group was starting to avoid.

Stona was cocky, brash, and disliked being proved wrong. Stona got into fights and often argued with his mother. For Anthony, whose own mother had abandoned him as child, seeing Kenneth argue with his mother triggered bad memories. Even when Kenneth and his mother argued from inside their home, Anthony could hear it and it bothered him. He couldn't bear the idea that someone could disrespect his own mother given all that she continued to do for him.

"You can't speak to your mama like that," Anthony would yell at Kenneth, several people restraining him. "I never had a mother, and you want to stand here and disrespect the woman who brought you into this world?" Anthony said while wiping the steady of flow of tears from his face. He couldn't fathom Kenneth's treatment of his mother.

Anytime Kenneth drank, he would fall into crippling insecurities—the same ones he had faced as a child. He reverted back to the wiry-framed boy who was the victim of teasing and bullying, and he would overcompensate by performing a brand of toughness. He became like the braggadocious rappers he watched in music videos, boasting about wealth and women and all the other fantasies he'd heard in rap songs. These were Kenneth's loneliest moments. The times when he was shunned by everyone he knew, left to resort to his only friends, the animals that he lived next to on the ranch.

Kenneth sprinted down the street to find Ebony at the convenience store, surrounded by Diego and a group of other homeless men. "Hi, gorgeous," Diego said while rubbing Ebony's coat.

The woman who worked at the cash register didn't mind that Kenneth tied up Ebony in her parking lot. Nor that Ebony left enormous droppings out front of her store because Kenneth frequented the store so often. Besides, the store next door sold farm animal feed and sometimes scooped up the manure to use as fertilizer.

As Kenneth rode west on Alondra Boulevard, he steered Ebony's reins in the direction of the incoming traffic. He was fearless and numb after the pain from the fight with KJ earlier that morning.

The sun shone brightly on his face. He closed his eyes and rode into the intersection, didn't open them until the cars started honking.

"I don't care!" he yelled. "This is my city!"

He had the look of someone who had reached a fork in the road. His daily quarrels had gotten the best of him, and maybe it was time to end it all, he thought to himself as he loosened Ebony's reins and urged her to move forward while cars continued to honk and swerve in and out of the street. When he returned home, he was greeted by the sight of Carlton, who was sound asleep on his living room couch. Outside, on the other side of his property, Kenneth's mother, Susan, was lamenting to Keenan.

"I think it's that girl that he always hangs with," she said. They were standing under a wooden canopy near the bleachers that overlooked the ranch. Susan was convinced his ex-girlfriend was one of the main sources of Kenneth's problems; after dating her for a year, he was left heartbroken.

Keenan nodded in agreement, kicked the dirt with his foot. He wasn't sure what to say. He knew the version of Kenneth that they had all been seeing wasn't the boy he met when they were young. He knew the real Kenneth and wanted him back like the rest of the cowboys did. "I've known him since he was fourteen," he said to Susan as a pack of dogs barked down the street. "I used to sleep over all the time, and I know the real him—he can't keep riding this wave. It's going to get him injured."

Susan agreed that being a part of the Compton Cowboys was one of the only things that was keeping Kenneth from completely going over the edge. It was the only hope she had to save her boy from complete self-destruction.

"I'm worried that he's going to mess up the whole Compton Cowboys thing," she said.

"Exactly," Anthony said as he dusted off the dirt from his work pants and walked up next to them.

"You guys have to have an intervention for him," his mother said.

Anthony and Keenan silently nodded in approval.

"Because if not, he's going to get hurt," she said as she wiped tears from her eyes. "He's going to get killed because he can be crazy."

Susan's tears summoned deep feelings in Anthony. He

reached over to hug her while thinking about his own mother.

"It's confusing for us, Susan, because when he drinks he wants to fight us and gets in our faces," Keenan said. "We're all friends and it should never come down to that, and then when he gets sober he always apologizes. We need Kenny back, the Kenny I used to know," he added, while Anthony nodded in agreement.

"You know Kevin, my husband, is from the South Side of Chicago, and he doesn't play any games," Susan continued after a long pause. "He was ready to evict him and hand him over to the police. But I fought him and said that he couldn't do that to my child. Kenny will tell me he's doing better and hasn't drank in five days, but then something will trigger him and will upset him."

"Oh, I didn't know that," Keenan said.

"It's that girl, I tell you, she just jerks him around."

"It messes with his head," Keenan responded.

"You guys have to save him. I've tried everything. Doctors, hospitals, clinics. You're his friends and he needs you," she said. "Yesterday, he called me and told me he was scared and couldn't be by himself. He's not going to survive alone," she added. "He was bullied as a kid and had to develop a tough guy image that he puts on sometimes."

"That's when Stona comes out," Keenan said. "The tough guy, his alter ego."

Anthony chimed in. "He don't know what being tough really means. I was raised in these streets. He never had to do any of that. He never had to steal because he had no money. He never had to rob nobody's car. He don't know nothing about this life."

"When he turns into Stona, he disappears. And when we call him Kenny he won't respond," Keenan added.

"Maybe that should be part of the intervention," Susan said. "I'm not going to pay for thirty-day rehab and put up that kind of money if he's not going to go to it."

"Right," Anthony said. "What's the point if he's not going to go to it?"

"That's a waste of money."

"We took him to one in Long Beach before. I had it all set up. Right on the beach, where he could have run every morning if he wanted to. They were going to give him a scholarship, but he had to detox and two days in he blew up on someone in there. He thought he was only going to go for a day but then got angry when he realized he was going to sleep there." Susan wiped more tears from her face. "But with the help of you guys and these horses, I think he still has a chance to be okay."

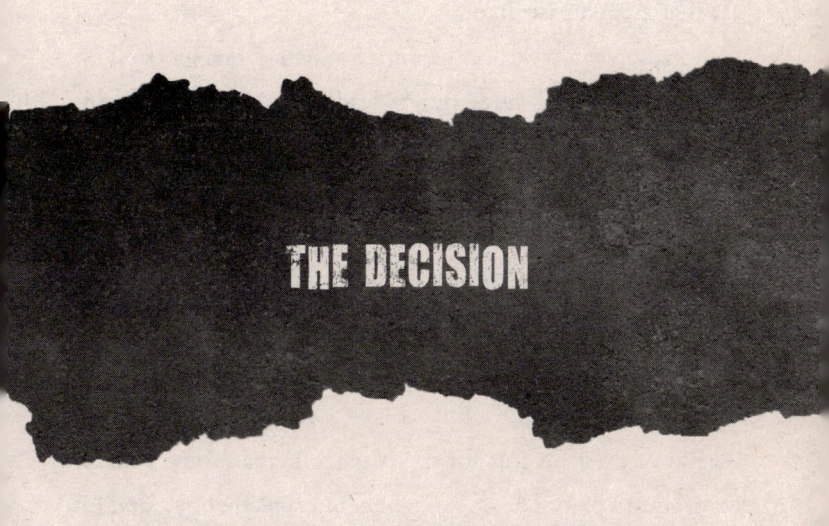

# THE DECISION

**THE CARS CONTINUED TO DRIVE** past Keenan and Terrance as both of their horses trotted north on Wilmington Boulevard in the midday sun. Since making a right onto the busy boulevard, their light conversation had shortened and their body language shifted. As the lead rider, it was Terrance's responsibility to make sure that the road was clear ahead. Keenan would have his eye on their rear.

Because of conflicting work schedules, it had been two months since they last rode together. Terrance hardly took days off from his job in Compton's waste services, and Keenan had moved to Inglewood with his wife and daughter months ago, making riding together that much more difficult.

In moments, Keenan's five-seven frame had gone from slightly slouched to fully erect, as he focused his gaze on each car that zipped past them.

It had been a few months since Sonny last got spooked on Wilmington Boulevard, nearly leading to a fatal accident, which had become a running joke in the cowboys' group text chat ever since. But it was far from comedic for Keenan, who continued to have nightmares about the experience.

For Terrance, who was almost five years older than Keenan, riding on Wilmington came with more risks. Terrance had been in the neighborhood longer and had a bigger reputation among the Nutty Blocc Crips. He had been on several of their hit lists for the damage he had done to their community before he was a member of the cowboys, and his slender face and six-foot-six frame were even harder to miss on a horse.

As they continued to trot, Sonny began to feel Keenan's nervousness and jumped at every passing car.

"Easy, Sonny," he whispered in his ear. "I'm just as scared as you are."

A minute later a black car with dark tinted windows slowed down next to the two friends and stopped in the middle of the street. As the car's windows rolled down, Keenan and Terrance immediately looked at each other and communicated in an unspoken language. Their first impulse was to immediately let the horse reins go, dig their shoes into their horses' sides, and sprint away toward safety. Horses could reach speeds of up to thirty miles per hour in a matter of seconds, and in dangerous situations, their horsepower proved more effective than even the fastest runner.

Or they could take their chances and stay.

Terrance and Keenan faced their horses in the direction of the ranch in case they had to make a quick escape. But once the tinted glass rolled down, it was a black woman in her early forties who met their gaze. She was alone in her car. Both of them eased and their blood pressure returned to normal.

"I love y'all so much! I love me some black cowboys!" she shouted from the inside of her black Mazda sedan as a pair of fuzzy black dice swung from the rearview mirror.

The two looked at each other and chuckled. *Crazy lady*, they thought, and continued to ride back toward the ranch.

"We love you, too," Terrance shouted as they rode away.


Tre sat in the living room later that same day watching a daytime courtroom television show.

He had been aimlessly scrolling on his phone for the past thirty minutes at his brother's home in Lynwood, waiting for the mother of his son, Logan, to call him. It had been over an hour, and he began to worry about her whereabouts. He hadn't seen his child in over two months, and the last time something like this happened, she had fled out of state with their son.

Their relationship had never recovered.

Tre had mixed feelings about being back in Compton. On one hand, it gave him the chance to be around his child again and the rest of the cowboys. But it also deprived him of being able to work on the Flying U Ranch full-time and compete in the rodeo circuit. He helped out at the cowboys' ranch, but it wasn't enough. Some days were easier than others. Though he had ambitions of competing again, his leg wasn't fully healed from a fight he'd gotten into. Doctors had advised him to stay off it for at least another three months.

In the meantime, he spent hours watching old footage of himself competing in bareback riding competitions, studying his posture and handling of the horse in the same way professional football players studied their opponent's footage before a big game. On the side of the television, near the old record player, were other DVDs of past competitions that he watched from time to time, but they were nowhere near as big as the stack he had at his grandmother's home. Tre was a student of the sport, and even though he wasn't physically fit to ride, being at home had given him the chance to watch his old footage and learn from his mistakes.

As the TV blared, Tre continued to scroll through his phone.

There were other things he could have been doing other than being at his brother's home. But then the screen on his phone suddenly changed and his father's name showed up.

"Hello?"

"Get to the 'hood right now," Tre's father said on the phone. His deep baritone voice echoed through Tre's ears. "Something just happened to Marcus. He got shot."

Before Tre had a chance to react to the news about his closest cousin, Tre's mother's door swung open across the room.

"Did y'all hear about Marcus?" she said. "Greg just called me and said he's at the burger stand where Marcus got killed."

Tre hung up the phone and sank deep into the couch. His body collapsed. He felt the weight of the world and none of it at the same time. Marcus had been like a big brother. He had always followed closely in his footsteps, and they were inseparable every time Marcus was out of prison.

Tre hobbled out of the house, still nursing the injured leg, while his brother sprinted out of the house. They jumped into his brother's car and headed to Spook Town. When they pulled up to Cypress Street ten minutes later, the entire neighborhood was blocked off by yellow tape and a police barricade. Police cars and a paramedic van assembled around the scene, their flashing red and blue lights barely visible in the daytime sun.

"That's my cousin over there!" Tre yelled as the police officers refused to let him past the yellow tape. He continued to yell as two officers denied him access to the crime scene. His cousin Daneisha had joined him. Tre looked at his brother, and without saying a word, he knew they needed to find a way around the police line. They both got back into the car and drove around the corner, parking several houses down. With the help of his brother, Tre managed to climb over two fences and traverse two lawns, finally getting to the scene of the crime through the back parking lot of the restaurant.

Marcus's body lay on the ground, covered by a white sheet in front of a group of palm trees near Tony's Burgers. There were small orange cones around his body and five police officers, two of whom wrote on a notepad. Some of the Spook Town Crips had also found a way to avoid the barricade and were now at the scene, alarming some of the police officers, who were afraid of immediate retaliation.

Some of the Spook Town Crips wore brown bandanas on their faces, exposing only their eyes, fearful that their identity would be revealed in front of the police officers, who often used murder scenes to photograph and bust suspected gang members.

At this point, the entire neighborhood had now gathered to honor Marcus's death.

Marcus had been out of prison for six months the day he was murdered on August 3, 2018. After serving two years in prison, his demeanor had changed. He trusted people less and confided only in himself and a small circle of intimate friends and family. He was supposed to be at work the day he was gunned down, but instead he called off to attend a friend's birthday dinner that evening. While washing his car in front of his home, two men approached him, and after a verbal exchange one of the men fired on Marcus and hit him in the abdomen. Wounded from the bullet, he continued to run around the corner to Willowbrook, where he was shot again and eventually passed out in the parking lot of Tony's Burgers.

He died minutes later on the only patch of green grass near the parking lot.

Marcus's death almost forced Tre to give up riding. It was these types of assaults—random, spontaneous, and personal— that made kids in the 'hood want to join gangs just to avenge the death of their loved ones. And in moments like this, Tre couldn't help but feel that tug as well. But throwing his rodeo dreams away also meant his cousin's son, now left behind, would also be without a male figure in his life. With Marcus's death, Tre knew he needed to step up as a father for his cousin, so he assumed the responsibility of helping raise his cousin's son. He wasn't going to let the streets take his life like they had Marcus's.

Word of Marcus's death spread fast throughout the farms. When Keenan first heard, he thought about his own friends and relatives who had passed.

As a child, Keenan knew death intimately; it was a

frequent visitor who often showed up unannounced, but when he turned thirteen he suddenly became immune to the sounds of wailing mothers who hugged the bodies of their lifeless children on the street. The scene became a reoccurring image that played throughout the day. His eyes grew accustomed to the vivid night rainbows that the paramedic lights created on the sides of homes—their colors, ironically, matching the same blue and red tones that people in the neighborhood were living and dying for.

Anthony experienced the same thing when he became a teenager. Terrance remembered it as a gradual process. Randy went through it, too, and so did Keiara. Around so much death, each of their bodies began to store trauma the way soldiers who fought in distant lands did, a form of post-traumatic stress.

These battlefields, however, were in Compton.

Some of their pain was internalized and locked away deep, only to surface years later in the middle of the night as screams and cold sweats. Some of their bodies hardened up and formed moats to fortify the space between their skin and the outside world—a tactic rooted in preservation and survival.

Keiara remembered the first time she woke up in the middle of the night, her first night terror following her brother's murder. The screams and the uncontrollable crying and the fits of rage that she unleashed on those closest to her.

**RIGHT:** Anthony is at home with his granddaughters. He rode his horse to pick one of them up at school. He tends to do this on Fridays. They live in the Imperial Courts Housing Projects in Watts, California.

**BOTTOM:** Anthony is at his grand-daughter's elementary school in Watts, California. All the kids are petting his horse, Dakota. He rode his horse from the Richland Farms ranch. It took about thirty minutes to get to the school.

**TOP:** Compton Cowboys members Charles Harris and Randy Hook are sitting on their horses during the middle of the Compton Christmas parade.

**BOTTOM:** Anthony is washing Dakota in the driveway. Every cowboy contributes to the grooming of the horses.

**TOP:** Keenan Abercrombia gets ready to start his day.

**BOTTOM:** Keenan rides through the streets of Compton, California.

Anthony is having a moment with his horse, Dakota, on the Richland Farms ranch. He works at the ranch every day from five a.m. to noon. Anthony takes care of all the horses but has the strongest bond with Dakota.

arlton Hook, Keenan Abercrombia, and Kenneth Atkins wait for their order of food to arrive 'om the local Louisiana Fried Chicken restaurant in Compton, California. (*New York Times*)

enneth waits for the light to turn green on his horse, Ebony. They are standing on the tersection of Wilmington and Alondra Boulevard.

Keiara and her daughter, Taylor, ride around the stables in nearby Gardena, California.

Tre Hosley's championship saddle.

Tre Hosley is breaking in a horse in Kenneth's backyard stable.

Randy Hook and Kenneth Atkins ride through the streets of Compton, California.

re Hosley tends to one of his horses on the Richland Farms ranch.

She didn't understand her pain until after the death of her younger brother. But growing up in Compton came with two choices: you toughened up, or you became a victim. Being vulnerable was never an option.

The biggest issue for the cowboys was learning how to cope with the way the horses helped heal them. Whereas horses were the physical cure that brought the cowboys together on the farms, their shared experiences of violence and trauma were the glue that bound them together, whether they wanted to admit it or not.

Randy often thought about Eugene, the young boy who admired the group and accompanied them in the parade. He was part of a different generation, but the times hadn't changed so much that the kid wouldn't face the same problems—he already had, in fact. The post-traumatic stress had started for Randy when he was Eugene's age, but it wasn't until his adult years and starting the Compton Cowboys that he could see that trauma from a distance. And that blindness, he felt, was the most dangerous part—when you're submerged in the violence around you, it becomes normalized, and you don't see how you're affected by it.

While the pain of loss and violence was almost unbearable, horses were often the answer to years of undiagnosed trauma. The horses allowed them to heal, to cope. They gave them a sense of purpose in the everyday routine of taking care of them. Randy recognized how lucky they were to have the horses and the ranch, that it was an outlet that most kids growing up in gang territories did not have. He believed that equine therapy helped him and his friends heal, and more so, that the horses healed from their own traumatic pasts as well. It was a give-and-take relationship. Most of their horses had experienced various forms of trauma. Some of them had abusive owners; others came from chaotic and careless environments.

The trauma the cowboys experienced brought them closer to understanding the horses they cared for. It created a symbiosis of love and care that continued to pave a pathway forward. Ultimately, it came down to trust. If a horse was traumatized and a cowboy was, too, an understanding of each other had to be forged over time. Randy felt that horses, like humans, were naturally gentle creatures, and if you nurtured them and fostered peace, you would find it, too. As Keenan would often say, "It's life or death, man."

# PASSING THE REINS

**ANTHONY SOFTLY UNLOCKED THE** three deadbolts in his front door while his son, Anthony Jr., was asleep on the couch, tired from playing video games the previous night.

It was an unseasonably cold morning for August. A mysterious cold front had come the night before, and the grass outside his home was partially frosted over. Every streetlight was still on in the Imperial Courts projects.

Anthony saw a group of young men just coming home from a party in the distance who reminded him of himself fifteen years ago. At thirty-six, however, he had different objectives. He was a family man, and waking up to work at the ranch early each morning was the only thing he cared about these days. After warming up his truck for ten minutes, he opened the door and stepped outside to place a pair of large orange public works cones in his parking spot. Assigned parking wasn't allowed in the projects, but nobody dared touch Anthony's cones.

He wiped his side rearview mirror with the outside of his shirt, rearranged his durag that he wore under his beanie, and drove in the direction of the ranch.

He'd kept the same morning routine since he first started working at the ranch seven years ago. This morning's drive was the same as others: quiet and contemplative. Outside of his time with the animals at the ranch, driving was one of the only activities that allowed him to be silent. The ten minutes in the truck gave him the chance to think about the duties he had to complete on the ranch that day.

The streets were relatively calm as Anthony drove on Wilmington Boulevard. Except for the sound of his rumbling truck and a few homeless men near the corner of Rosecrans, the streets were desolate, almost postapocalyptic. But in just a few hours they would be filled with black and brown faces on their way to work or school.

Anthony arrived at the ranch minutes before five a.m., put his car in park, and turned off the engine. He waited for a few minutes in his truck and scrolled through Instagram, catching up on messages he hadn't responded to from the previous night. The idea that Instagram could allow him to see what other people were doing around the world astounded him as he swiped through people's stories and posts. To him, who had almost never traveled outside Compton, it was crazy that he could be on the ranch and simultaneously speaking to people all over the world.

Anthony had always worked with his hands. His father, a retired mechanic, had taught him that manual labor was as close to God's work as one could get. Picking up large bales of hay to feed the horses and shoveling their droppings were difficult tasks, but he completed them with ease. After all, the ranch had to be in top shape when the kids program began again early next year. The ranch relied entirely on donations and grants from donors, and it was important to them to have a vibrant youth program. The money that previous donors had left was running out, and if things didn't change soon, Anthony would be out of a job.

When January ended, there was still no sign of the children Randy had promised. Anthony's mornings continued as they had been, but something about the ranch felt different. He now had two extra horses to look after, taking up two more stalls, bringing them to almost full capacity. The only thing missing from the ranch now was the sound of children cleaning the stalls and riding horses for the first time.

But the children never showed. At thirty-six, and the eldest member of the cowboys, it was Anthony's dream not only to give back to the ranch that had saved his life, but also to keep the ranch running for future generations. He worried that some of the younger guys were getting too caught up in the image of the Compton Cowboys rather than giving back to the community. And the clock was ticking—Mayisha had given them a year to prepare for a rejuvenation of their old programs, and with dwindling funds and resources, who knew if that would even be enough time.

After Anthony cleaned the stalls that morning, some of Mayisha's old friends showed up. Anthony straightened up and waved hello. His white tank top was drenched with sweat and dirt marks from the trailer that he had been cleaning for the past hour. Seeing Mayisha was a rare sight at the ranch these days since she had moved. She had been back only to handle financial matters, and she almost never came alone. She was usually accompanied by old friends and people who had volunteered on the ranch throughout the years.

Today was no different.

An unknown white woman and man accompanied her assistant, Kathy, a longtime volunteer, to the horse stalls. They carried clipboards with them and documents while inspecting some of the horses. Anthony took a break from cleaning the trailer to see the transaction. It wasn't the first time Mayisha had sold horses or ranch equipment. When money was low, a horse would go. Sometimes two. Other times it would be a trailer. Every time Mayisha and her friends showed up to the ranch, something went missing. This time, one of the trailers that had been used to transport horses over the years was up for sale.

The ranch was slowly becoming a shadow of what it once was as Mayisha's retirement party drew closer and closer. As things disappeared, questions about the fate of the ranch began to grow within the cowboys' circle.

Keenan had arrived at the ranch minutes after the group had showed up.

"What's up, man?" Keenan said to Anthony, who continued to watch the group now in Sonny's stall, inspecting him for what they believed could be an eventual sale.

"You know Mayisha wants to sell the horses?" Anthony said to Keenan. They both leaned on the gate, watching the transaction take place before their eyes. "Kathy told me they want to sell Sonny. You better buy him before they can do that."

Keenan's body tensed up. Selling Sonny would mean losing another horse in his life.

"Oh no," Keenan responded. "I already talked to her about buying him a while ago, so I don't know what they're doing over there."

"It feels like they don't want to see us win," Anthony said.

Tensions on the ranch were escalating between the old guard and the new generation. More and more of the elder Compton Jr. Posse volunteers were now part of the transition team, and it was their job to ensure that nothing was left behind. Their duties were to help sell as many things as possible, even including Mayisha's home.

The cowboys, on the other hand, had different plans.

"I already bought Koda a few months ago," Anthony said. "I suggest you do the same for Sonny."

Keenan nodded and agreed.

# THE PARTY

**THE EVENT PLANNERS ARRIVED** at the ranch much earlier than expected on the morning of Mayisha's retirement party. The tent was all set up and covered the entire arena, creating a large shaded area for people to sit under. There were more than three hundred invitations sent out weeks before, and nearly two hundred people had RSVP'd. Valet parking attendants began to arrive at ten a.m.

Inside the ranch, the smell of Jamaican food and barbecue filled the air while a black grill blew hot steam out from its sides. Slowly, more people began to show up. The donors—who had supported Mayisha's vision of providing children from Compton with horses as an alternative to gangs and violence—were all in attendance. Their hair had grayed over the years and some of them needed help walking, but all were buoyed by their own memories of the ranch.

Like Mayisha, they, too, were there to announce that they would no longer be a part of the ranch's operations. They were retiring along with her.

Teal and yellow ribbons adorned each of the tables, with bouquets of flowers that matched the color scheme. On a typical day, the ranch embodied an image of toughness that was in stark contrast to the mood of the event, with its coordinated flowers and color scheme. The red carpet made the day feel like a spectacle, and the feeling of sanctuary the ranch gave so many members of the community was lost.

Randy and the rest of the cowboys wore their best outfits. Their collared shirts were tucked in, their Stetson hats were crisp, and their boots had just been shined. They looked like the images of black cowboys that they had wanted to see as children. Tre, in particular, wore his Bill Pickett championship belt with pride. It shined under the sun and reflected bright blue and gold colors in the eyes of whoever stood in front of him. Since the death of Marcus, Tre had been spending less time on the ranch and wearing his belt less, but that day, he held his shoulders back and his head to the sky as he walked on the red carpet and into the tent, eager to boast about how well he had done for himself in the rodeo world since the donors last saw him as a teenager.

Mayisha's contribution to the community was irreplaceable, but with the passing of the ranch operations to Randy, the community now had to rely on him for direction. Handshakes were exchanged between old friends and new friends.

When everyone sat down to eat, an MC got onstage and welcomed everyone to the event. She spoke of the impact that Mayisha had on the community and the hole that her exit would be leaving. Mayisha sat near the back of the tent with her partner, Jody, a longtime volunteer.

The couple were both now well into their sixties and had lived through some of the worst and best times at the ranch. As they held hands on top of the table, they remembered their first parade and the looks on people's faces as they proudly rode in unison. They also remembered the gang wars that had taken so many young black lives in the 1990s. They remembered the bullets that found a home in some of their riders. Those days were the hardest until Jody, a military veteran, made a decision.

"I put my body on the line for my country. Why shouldn't I do the same thing for my community?" he told Mayisha, remembering the bullets that zipped by his head one night during one of the gang wars.

The words that the speakers shared that afternoon described a glorious past, one filled with great challenges and rewarding outcomes. It was supposed to be a party, but it felt like a celebration of a bygone era.

The future of the ranch was uncertain, and everyone in attendance looked at the cowboys for answers that they did not have. Speaking about the future felt taboo, and until Randy stepped onstage, not a word was said about it.

When Randy hopped onto the stage, he kissed his aunt on the cheek and complimented her on her yellow West African kente cloth dress.

"I'm so proud of my aunt," he said while smiling to the crowd. "I'm so proud to be able to continue her legacy. Most important, I'm proud to be a cowboy."

He spoke of the journey that they had embarked on as children and the process by which they had arrived at this moment.

"We're in the process of developing five different programs for the ranch," he said while members in the audience clapped cautiously, skeptical of this plan. "It's going to be called the Compton Jr. Equestrians and will include skills training and clinical therapy for our youth. We want to see this work in Compton and then use it as a model for other 'hoods in the U.S. and around the world."

After the party ended, Randy talked with some donors he had known since he was a child. They congratulated him and were eager to hear about his plans in greater detail. The idea to replicate the ranch model was something Mayisha hadn't envisioned. Her mission was to save Compton's youth, but Randy had more far-reaching dreams.

"I'm trying to get the ranch running smoothly with the hopes of taking this model and applying it in different cities across the U.S.," he said while adjusting his belt buckle. "We're connected to cowboys in Philadelphia, black cowboys in Chicago, and also with cowboys overseas. We just need the resources to do this in a big way and put ranches like this one in inner-city environments where there's a lack of nature, because we see that this model works."

A group of four white donors looked at Randy with curiosity. Here was a young man with big dreams but no proven track record. The model would be hard to accomplish, but before he could expand, he would first have to find a way to keep this ranch alive.

"What makes you so confident that this model would work somewhere else?" an elderly woman in a blue dress asked.

"Because we believe in the horses and their ability to make everything better. They changed us, and we think they can have the same effect on at-risk youth everywhere." This was Randy's core belief.

# BACK AT THE RANCH

**IT HAD BEEN ONLY** a couple of months since Mayisha saw Anthony at her retirement party, but she walked up to him and looked at him like she hadn't seen him in years. Her grayish hair was covered by a turquoise-and-black hat that shielded just enough of her face to keep the sun away.

"Hi, Mama!" Anthony yelled, running toward Mayisha while Keenan and Terrance followed closely behind. "Oh . . . youuu look good!" he said, examining her physique the way someone would do after not seeing their old friend for a while. "You put on some weight, Mama! Jody been feeding you good, I see!"

Anthony did another full circle around Mayisha,

continuing to laugh hysterically. "You loooooking good."

Mayisha smiled and blushed, her light brown cheeks lightening up in the sun. She glanced down at her tight black pants and red toenails. "Oh yeah, you know," she replied in a soft tone while continuing to laugh. "I'm doing okay."

Since her retirement party, Mayisha had been spending less time on the ranch. When she did come to pick up mail or see her children, she took things back to her home in Riverside County. Some days it would be a horse, other days it would be equipment from the ranch. Her home was on the market, and though she had plans to sell the property soon, her one-year lease was coming to an end in Norco, forcing her to rethink her plans.

"Anthony, I need you do to me a favor," Mayisha asked after the laughter subsided. "Can you bring me six of those grooming kit buckets?"

"Six?" Anthony replied in a sarcastic tone.

"Yeah, I got a buyer," she responded.

Anthony nodded and walked back to the tack room accompanied by Terrance to find the grooming kits, leaving Keenan and Mayisha in the driveway. The two cast shadows behind them as they walked together toward the back of the ranch, the same way they had done since they were teenagers. Their waist sizes had slightly increased, but their pants still hung loosely on their legs.

As Anthony rummaged through the equipment, he

noticed that things in the room were dwindling by the day. Mayisha's plans to help other horseback-riding programs in her new neighborhood were evident, but at the current rate there would be no ranch equipment left in the tack room for the Compton Cowboys' own youth program.

Keenan anxiously pointed his toe in the gravel and put his hands beneath his black Compton Cowboys sweater while they waited for Anthony to return. "You know I'm back now?" he said without making eye contact with Mayisha.

Mayisha looked up at him.

"You're back?" she asked, surprised.

"Yeah, the rent was getting too high in Inglewood, so we had to move back."

Mayisha looked at him and ruffled through her bag with one of her hands, searching for her phone.

"But we're doing good now," he said, raising his voice. "We're back on it and making sure things run smoothly around here."

"Mmm-hmm," Mayisha responded with the same speculation that a loving mother would have of a child who hadn't yet shown that they were capable of changing a bad habit.

The last time she and Randy had spoken, they had disagreed over the day-to-day operations of the ranch and the image that the cowboys were portraying to the outside world. She believed that the cowboys were more interested in self-promotion than they were in giving back to their community; riding around the neighborhood with sandals and bareback was a departure from the values she had fought tirelessly to uphold. Mayisha had expressed how they could be of great value to the community, but she wasn't yet convinced that they were interested in running the program. She believed that the cowboys' best chance for survival was to try to build the relationships that she had created with the wealthy donors. She felt that the inability to continue the program had more to do with a generational gap, a "disappointment that black parents had" when their children couldn't continue the work that they had done for the previous generation.

*If they were smart*, she thought, *they would continue to ride English*. It would bring them into a different economic level, and there were just more connections and funding in that world. She believed that the clean-cut, conservative aspects of riding English were what brought respect to her program in the first place. She wished that such a legacy would continue, but that was the biggest challenge for the cowboys. It was February, and only four children had showed up to the first orientation. Money was running low, and the idea of limiting Anthony's work hours had begun to circulate through Randy's mind. Establishing the youth program was their largest concern, but finding the resources to sustain it was critical.

# COWBOY BEEF

**"HEY, YOU FROM THE** Compton Cowboys?" a voice asked Kenneth while he pulled on two wire cables at the gym.

The unknown man stood a few feet behind him while he finished his set.

He asked again, but this time he grabbed Kenneth's shoulder and gestured that he should take off his headphones.

The man was in his mid-forties and had prison tattoos all over his body. His lifted chest and forty-five-degree-angle-pointed feet, one slightly hidden behind the other, signaled that he was from the streets.

"Are you part of the Compton Cowboys?" he asked again. A friend of his had now joined him, standing almost the same way.

Both waited for a response.

"Yeah, I am," Kenneth finally responded while he put the weights back down on the floor and took his headphones off. His own shoulders tightened up and his chest bulked in front of him, ready for confrontation.

"I'm from Compton and a member of the hill riders, and my boys and I don't like the way y'all are representing black cowboys," the man said while rubbing his hands together in front of his chest. "Y'all look like clowns wearing sandals when you ride."

The two men were black horseback riders who were part of another black horseback-riding group on the hill, a horse ranch located in South Central that had burned down in 2012.

Riders from the hill were some of the first black urban cowboys in Southern California who had helped create the riding area in the 1960s. Like the ranch on the farms, the hill became an oasis for black riders in South Central who arrived from the South. Within a matter of years, the hill had grown into a thriving horseback-riding community and, like the ranch, gave African-American youth like Tre and Keiara a place to congregate and ride horses at a time when the pressure to join gangs continued to take the lives of many. In 2012, however, the hill mysteriously burned down late one night in a suspected case of arson. The fire deeply impacted the lives of many of its riders, causing Keiara and Tre to move their horses to the ranch. The others who were left without a place to house their horses were forced to sell.

Kenneth backed up from the two men and braced himself for a fight.

"You think kids in the 'hood are going to respect y'all when y'all acting like clowns?" the man asked.

Since the cowboys first officially banded together, they had been criticized for not always wearing traditional cowboy clothing when they rode through the streets of Compton. Older generations of riders from the hill, like the man who stood in front of Kenneth, believed it was disrespectful and portrayed the wrong image of black cowboy culture.

"We don't have to wear tucked-in shirts and baggy jeans with our boots," Kenneth explained. "We have our own style and our own way of doing things."

The conversation continued with no end in sight. The difference in generational views about cowboy culture wasn't going to get solved that day, and Kenneth knew he couldn't fight both of them. He needed Randy to be there.

"Hold up, let me call my homie," Kenneth told them. "He'll be able to explain what we're trying to do."

Cowboy beef had also become a growing concern in Compton. Like the Compton Cowboys, who were from a Crip neighborhood, riders from the hill lived in a neighborhood full of Piru Bloods. They were linked by blood and affiliation, which didn't end when they mounted their horses.

When Randy arrived at the gym, the four walked out to a quiet part of the parking lot, where he and Kenneth prepared for the unexpected.

"I done had people I know die for this Compton horse life," the man said while raising his voice, creating a scene as people walked in and out of the gym. His passion and love for horses were evident as his voice echoed throughout the parking lot. "I'm a real cowboy, and we put our hats on and boots and go roping and y'all making us look bad."

The older cowboy's issue stemmed from the media attention that the Compton Cowboys had been receiving over the past year. He felt that they hadn't paid their dues and were riding on the coattails of the legacy established by riders from the hill. The energy that he brought to the conversation was the same that could be seen throughout the city of Compton. It was rough and raw and intense.

To an outsider, four black men standing in a parking lot facing one another could have resembled a fight about gang territory, women, or drugs. But the conversation was entirely about horses and cowboys. They went back and forth, and it was clear that neither side wanted to fight. The elder just wanted to communicate his concern for the future of black cowboys in Compton.

"We just have a different approach," Randy explained to both riders from the hill. "We're not new to Compton. I'm born and raised on the farms. My whole family is from the farms, and my auntie has been doing this since before we were born."

Slowly the man's tense posture eased up. The look in his eyes went from anger to understanding as he continued to take in Randy's words.

"I done buried two of my homies this past year," Randy explained. "We're really about this 'hood and cowboy life."

The conversation deescalated after each man explained his stance. Neither cowboy was right or wrong, and the altercation instead reflected a broader issue that was affecting black cowboys across Los Angeles. Older riders were becoming increasingly disconnected from the younger generation of black cowboys. When older black riders first began riding, they experienced discrimination and rejection. They had to look twice as good and ride three times better than the average white cowboy in order to be taken seriously. It's the reason why black rodeo competitions like the Bill Pickett Invitational Rodeo were started in the first place. But the younger generation of riders was bringing their own style and customs to horseback riding. In other words, they were taking ownership.

The talk opened up a conversation that Randy had been meaning to have with other black riders in and around Compton. The showdown became the perfect opportunity for the leader of the Compton Cowboys to shatter the stereotypes that people had about them. The suggestion of organizing a riding event together was raised as a way to unite both groups. Riding together, they believed, would help create better bonds with other riders, and it would also help the older generation understand the mission that Randy and his friends were on. Like the riders from the hill, the Compton Cowboys were on a mission to eradicate stereotypes about black cowboys and reinsert themselves and others into the history books.

Kenneth, on the other hand, couldn't let the situation go that easily. The two men had rubbed him the wrong way and confirmed that he was one of the most hated cowboys in Compton. Other black riders thought he was a joke, and that didn't sit well with him.

"There's Blood and Crip beef in the 'hood, but this is cowboy beef," he said as he drove away from the group toward the ranch.

Keenan took a long look around the ranch. There was still a lot of work to do before the guys showed up, and if he hurried he could feed all the horses and clean some of the stalls in the next hour.

He filled up each stall with hay. It had been almost two weeks since he had fully moved back to Compton from Inglewood, and the ranch hand life was starting to become routine to him once again. When he was working at a restaurant in downtown Los Angeles, an average weekend commute would take him almost an hour. But since he had begun to work as the weekend ranch hand, his commute was only a few steps.

"You looking good today," he told Sonny, diving his head deep inside the hay feeder in his stall. "Eat all the hay you can while it's dry, 'cause the rain might come back later."

Tre and Mike both lay on their backs on Tre's car in the driveway while they waited for other members of the cowboys to show up. The two wide-shouldered former football players and single fathers had been spending more time together these days. In his free time, Tre had begun cutting hair and had booked an appointment with Keenan.

Since the youth program wasn't in full operation yet, weekends on the ranch had been quiet over the past few months. But since Kenneth had been approached at the gym by riders from the hill, certain members of the cowboys had different opinions about which action to take, prompting an informal meeting at the ranch that day.

In a surprising turn of events, one of the hill riders actually extended an invitation to a group ride with other black cowboys in two weeks. The ride would also include other black riding groups from Southern California, and if everyone who was invited showed up, it would be one of the largest gathering of black cowboys in recent years.

The invitation was enticing, but not enough for Kenneth, who preferred to skip it, arguing instead that the hill riders "wanted to steal their clout" and try to ride the wave of attention that the cowboys had been receiving since they officially banded together more than two years ago.

"Them guys from the hill aren't from the farms," he said. "They're jealous of us because we can wake up in the morning and ride our horses. They can't do that because they don't have a ranch like us."

Anthony and Terrance's views aligned more with Kenneth's. As two of the oldest and most connected to the street life that they were actively trying to leave behind, their views were more aggressive.

"We can handle the situation whatever way they want to," Anthony said. "They mad 'cause we're younger than they are, but I can bring the chopper to the ride if necessary."

The threat of gun violence to settle the issues with the hill cowboys worried Randy. His hope to unite all black cowboys would be shattered if problems with the hill continued, and a war between the hill and the farms would automatically incite a war between members of the Bloods and Crips.

Marriah, the mother of Randy's child, Lux, appeared from the periphery, pushing Lux's gray stroller into the back of the ranch where the cowboys were sitting. He eventually got out and started walking around the group. The more time his son spent with the horses, the happier Randy became. Horses were becoming a big part of his life, and his comfort level with them was increasing rapidly. It also assured Randy that the Hook tradition of horse riding would continue.

As the young parents supervised their only son, Tre wrapped a barber's robe around Keenan, who was sitting on a makeshift stool that had been a part of the ranch for decades. Because the rodeo circuit didn't begin for another three months, Tre had recently gotten into cutting hair as way to pick up a new skill and make money. He began by cutting his own hair, which later transitioned into working on close friends and family. He didn't charge most of the cowboys, and took only what they could afford, but cutting hair was more than a hobby for him. Weeks before cutting Keenan's hair, he had enrolled in barber college, paying the $1,500 initiation fee with the hope of being officially licensed in the state of California.

The temperature continued to drop as the sun faded in the afternoon, and the guys paced the ranch grounds in order to stay warm. Keenan's wife had recently joined the group and stood next to Marriah while she braided a horse's hair.

When Keiara's black Chevrolet Suburban pulled up to the ranch, the group had already been hanging out for hours. Ever since she moved Penny from the Gardena stables to the ranch weeks before to save money, she had been spending more time with the cowboys, even though her injury continued to hinder her ability to ride.

"What's up, Kika?" everyone said as she and Taylor walked up to the group.

"Hiiiiiiiii, pretty little girrrrrrrrrrllllll," Keenan said from the barber chair, pointing at Taylor.

"Taylor, say hi to Keenan," Keiara told Taylor.

At this point in her life, Taylor had been around horses as much as she had been around humans. She waved at the group and immediately walked back to the stables searching for Penny.

The altercation with the hill cowboys was a bit more complicated for Tre and Keiara than it was for the rest of the cowboys. Both had first learned how to ride on the hill and were still connected to the riders. Though the hill was only a fraction of what it once had been since it burned down in 2012, for Keiara, it reminded her of the days she had spent there with her previous horse and her brother when they were still alive. But like the rest of the cowboys, she had mixed views about the new generation of riders who claimed to be from the hill.

That the hill was going through its own transformation wasn't a concern for the group. They, too, were in the process of creating a new vision for black cowboys from the farms. The deeper issue lay in the image that the Compton Cowboys were creating. Word from the black riding community was that several other black cowboy groups throughout California had issues with the way that the Compton Cowboys were carrying themselves, and not having the support of other black cowboys would hinder what the Compton

Cowboys were trying to create.

"I would love to be unified with other black cowboys," Randy said to the group as his black cap and black Ray-Ban sunglasses concealed his eyes and most of his face. "But the Willie Lynch theory is a real thing in the 'hood. Black people always finding ways to hate against one another, it's too common and we try to knock each other down. If we show up to the ride and there's beef with them, then that's just that Willie Lynch stuff happening."

The idea that black cowboys could quarrel, according to Randy, derived from a speech given by a slave owner in the early 1700s named Willie Lynch. The speech detailed a "secret" he had found—that is, the idea to separate enslaved Africans from one another in an effort to pit them against one another. The theory resonated with the group, including Bryson, a childhood friend who had shown up to the ranch that day with a bag full of oxtails for Keenan to cook later that night. He firmly nodded in agreement.

"We're just different from those guys," Kenneth said while sitting as far away from the alcohol as possible. "We ain't gotta wear cowboy boots all the time and—"

Randy immediately interjected.

"Yeah, we're different, but there's a movement that we're trying to create with them as well. And things like Instagram have helped us promote that culture. The goal has always been for every black cowboy to come out of the shadows.

Black cowboys have been around for years, but they haven't had the energy that we have, and we're trying to break all the barriers."

Nearly everyone nodded.

"Definitely," Keenan said while looking at his hair in a small mirror that Tre had put in front of his face.

Kenneth was the only one who didn't nod, still visibly upset about the way he had been approached by the hill riders.

In spite of the problems that were being addressed that day, the mood of the ranch had shifted. Whereas conventional wisdom might have suggested that Kenneth's past actions would have given his friends a reason to isolate him even further from the group, the incident did almost the exact the opposite: it brought them closer together. At one point, Randy went to the back shed and brought out two boards with older photos of the cowboys when they were members of the Compton Jr. Posse. It was something that he liked to do whenever the cowboys got together to remind everyone where they had come from. Each photo on the board told a different story. It reminded the cowboys of the bond that they had shared since they were children.

Everyone gathered around it.

"There goes Slim," Carlton pointed out while holding Lux in his arms. "And his mama, too." Since Slim had passed away months ago, photos and memories were all they had of the brother they had lost. Another photo showed Randy on his childhood horse named Lookattime, a white Arabian horse that was donated to the ranch from the University of Southern California's spirit squad.

A photo of Marriah and Randy sitting on a fence at the ranch brought back memories of the past fifteen years that they had shared together. The birth of Lux had brought them back together, but it also brought new challenges.

Keenan took off his robe, got up from the stool, and crouched down to look at the photos of their youth.

"Dang, you were a chicken head," he said to Marriah, who was wearing a red hooded sweater to cover her hair in the photo. "I remember that day," he continued. "That's when you and Randy first met."

"Me? A chicken head? Man, your horses are some chicken heads," she said, making the entire group roar with laughter. She looked directly at Keenan, who didn't have a response.

Randy quickly responded in defense of Keenan and the horses.

"Yeah, okay, maybe, but how we got one of the top hair stylists in the game that lives on the ranch? And these horses can't get no love? It doesn't make no sense!"

**RANDY WOKE UP WITH EVERYTHING** to be happy about the morning of the PBR event. A few prominent black bull riders were outside in the ranch arena visiting with other members of the cowboys and speaking about their shared interests and love for the sport.

He and the rest of the cowboys had just been invited to the Professional Bull Riding finals at the Staples Center in downtown Los Angeles the day before and were treated like superstars as they walked around the arena to standing ovations. The cowboys were becoming the ambassadors for black cowboys in ways that they had only dreamed about.

But something was off with Randy.

While the group of black bull riders from Texas continued to speak with Tre outside his bedroom, Randy was alone in his room having an emotional breakdown. Tears flowed from his eyes down his face onto his shoulders as he sat on the brown carpet floor wearing nothing but underwear, holding his head with two hands. The inside of his room was quiet, only catching some of the sounds of loud rap music that blasted in a car outside on the driveway, in competition with thousands of thoughts that filled his head.

There was just so much going on. He felt the weight and pressure of the ranch's troubles mounting, and with every small victory, the relief that followed was only temporary. It was enough to make someone go crazy. He kept going back to his family, thinking about how the Hook legacy was all on the line, and how he didn't want to disappoint them. He was figuring things out day to day—the business, the public relations, the guys, and the fate of the ranch.

The tears continued for the next thirty minutes. On the eve of their second day at the PBR event, the support that he and the cowboys received was hard to process. It was almost like a weird form of guilt, like they didn't deserve it. Being from Compton, they were so used to being antagonized that it suddenly felt surreal for people to accept them. He had to keep it together, keep from getting lost in the attention that circled around them. But he didn't know what to tell people who wanted to help—like Mayisha, he, too, was now struggling to let go of control and let other people in.

When the tears subsided, he wiped his face with a towel. His black cowboy hat and freshly pressed black Compton Cowboys T-shirt sat on his bed next to his signature gold watch, necklace, and bracelet. He put these on and came back to life, surveying himself in the mirror.

"I ain't playing with these guys," he said, smiling. "I ain't playin'."

Outside, Tre and Ezekiel Mitchell, a twenty-one-year-old professional bull rider from Texas, stood in the center of the arena while Keenan trained Sonny and Fury. The two competitors had more in common than they had differences. Both had grown up playing football and had come from low-income homes separated only by the thousands of miles between Ezekiel's small town in Texas and Tre's Compton.

As some of the only black competitors in a mostly white sport, the two instantly formed a brotherhood that stemmed from learning how to compete in their sports by studying and watching YouTube videos.

"Do you know Chris Byrd?" Ezekiel asked.

"Chris?" Tre yelled, laughing. "Man, I went to high school with that fool!"

They both laughed and recognized just how small the

black cowboy world was. At twenty-one, Ezekiel was considered one of the top ten riders internationally and on pace to becoming the best rider in the world.

"Y'all ready to go?" Randy said as he stepped out of his house. The cowboys had to head back to the PBR event, this time to attend a workshop about black cowboys and to meet Charles Sampson, a local hero from Watts, one of the greatest black bull riders of all time.

The cowboys' eyes widened as hall of famer Charles Sampson spoke about his experience growing up in Watts.

"Now we all know that Watts and Compton are very unattractive places to a lot of people in the world," he said to a group of about thirty black cowboys in attendance for the private workshop. "But even though I was from Watts and was often the only black competitor, I felt like I had to fit in. All I cared about was becoming the best bull rider I could be. Just like the ones from Texas and Oklahoma," he added.

Eugene, the youngest member of the cowboys, clung to every word that Charles said. "That sounds like me," he said, when learning that Charles's introduction to rodeo was riding ponies in and around Compton. He sat on the edge of his seat as Charles spoke about his success in the professional bull-riding circuit. Being the first African-American to win the Professional Rodeo Cowboys Association world championship in 1982 was no small feat. Neither was his induction into the hall of fame in 1996.

For Eugene, who came from a riding family of his own, meeting Charles Sampson was a dream. He looked around at the transformation of the Staples Center from a basketball arena into a riding arena and wondered about his own future. His family had ridden horses in Mississippi, and they were always present in his childhood; to compete in the PRCA as a calf roper had become his personal goal.

What the cowboys saw in Eugene was a younger version of themselves. Eugene was at an age when horseback riding helped him cope with the dangers of the streets. They saw a version of themselves they could mentor and teach.

For Eugene, the importance of the ranch had become crystal clear. He had found a new home there, a place that liberated him from all outside forces and influences. There were no worries on the ranch, just complete freedom.

Moments later, Randy raised his hand to ask Charles a question.

"What are you most excited about the state of black cowboy culture?" he asked.

"What am I most excited about?" Charles responded. He took a moment before replying, mulling over the question.

"It's you guys," he finally said.

# THE KIDS

**KEENAN RAN HIS TATTOOED** hands into the wooden garden bed outside his mother's home. It was still early, but harvest season was on the horizon. Every weed that he dug out from the garden was placed in a growing pile by his feet. His fingers slowly ran through the soil looking for the smaller weeds while continuing to massage them back into the dirt. This time next year, they would be eating the vegetables that grew from this garden.

It had been months since he had moved back in with his mother from the apartment that he shared in Inglewood with his wife and stepdaughter. The rising cost of living in Inglewood, coupled with his unemployment, had forced the young family to move back to Compton. Living back on the farms would be a departure from the life he and his wife had imagined for themselves, but being back on the ranch was also a way to save money, especially as their first child was due in only six months.

Being back on the ranch would also bring him closer to realizing his dream of opening up an agricultural plot of land with his friend Mike in Lancaster, who owned a few acres. They wanted to grow their own vegetables in order to bring back fresh produce to Compton on a weekly basis. After all, the Mexicans were growing their own vegetables and milking their own cows. Why couldn't they do that, too? The way Keenan imagined it, they could do that for the kids when more of them started coming back to the ranch.

As a chef, he understood the importance of food and healthy eating. He was brought up in a food desert with unequal access to healthy food and vegetables. He wanted to change that, and giving his community access to healthier lifestyles could impact their physical health. He couldn't believe that most people had no idea where their food came from, or that they'd never experienced the satisfaction of growing their own food. People who shopped at stores didn't know the whole process. On top of the vegetables that he would grow, living back on the ranch would help him fully commit to the ranch's survival.

As he tended his garden, he heard the sounds of a few children in the arena who were there for Saturday classes.

Their voices reminded him of the past, when the ranch was full with as many as fifty kids at any given time.

He listened to the children, thinking about the future of the ranch.

Twelve-year-old Ethan sat next to his brother, Isaiah, and waited for his turn to answer the questions that were written in front of him on his worksheet. They were accompanied by Star and Lauren, two middle schoolers who lived minutes away from the ranch.

"If something gets stuck in its intestine, they can die from overeating," Ethan said to the group, reading attentively from his worksheet. The two brothers had been part of the Compton Jr. Posse in years past, but it was one of their first times back on the ranch and with Jamie, a CJP alumnus, who had since taken over the Saturday morning sessions.

Star read from the worksheet and learned about horses in ways that her local Compton school district didn't have the resources to provide her with.

"If something gets stuck in the intestine," she read while the sound of a police helicopter above the ranch suddenly drowned out her voice, "the horse will get . . ."

She stopped reading and looked up at sky while the helicopter made its way over the ranch and flew in the direction of the courthouse. At this point in their lives, everyone in the circle understood that when the helicopters got too loud, it was time to take a break from reading.

Nearby, in Fury's stable, Randy groomed his horse while his son played in the front house with his mother as she did someone's hair. He looked at the children and smiled. The youth program was slowly returning to the ranch, and although there weren't as many children as there once were, it was something, nonetheless. What Randy worried about, however, was how to attract more at-risk youth in the community—the type of children who would benefit the most from the program. That was critical, not just for the ranch but for Compton. Many of the younger riders had left when the ranch converted to English-style riding, but Randy was determined to rein them back in. Those were the kids who needed the most healing.

At this point, maintaining a positive attitude was all Randy could do, since the large donations he had hoped to secure had not come through, making the ranch's future more precarious than ever. Smaller donations, ranging from hundreds of dollars to several thousand, were not enough to sustain the ranch, which as of recently had cost almost twenty-five thousand dollars a month to maintain.

Each child stared at Randy as the helicopter sounds subsided and he finished grooming his horse, preparing her for a ride around the neighborhood. Star, the eleven-year-old daughter of a Mexican mother and African-American father, smiled and stared the hardest when he walked Fury out into the street.

Next to her, an intense debate was occurring.

"They can definitely die from overeating," Jamie said to Ethan and Isaiah, who had since begun a debate about whether a horse's ability to poop impacted its chances for survival.

"They can't poop when they . . ." Jamie said before being cut off by an overzealous Ethan, whose large bifocals were tucked deep into his worksheet.

"Dude, it starts with a *c*," he told Isaiah, still searching for the answer in his worksheet and struggling to remember the name of one of the horse's intestinal parts that aided with digestion.

"You mean the cecum?" Jamie finally responded after playfully laughing at the two brothers' brief exchange. "You guys are funny," she added.

Jamie took the group into the arena and grabbed a couple of grooming kits from the shed.

"You guys know the safety rules, right?" she said. "Go grab your helmets and put your boots on, too."

"Are we going to ride with saddles or bareback?" Ethan asked.

"Bareback," she said with a smile.

Although Jamie had mostly learned to ride English style, there was no escaping the influence of the Compton style of bareback riding that those before her had taken on in the farms. It was a tradition.

Lauren was reluctant as she stood by Ethan while he

brushed Chocolate's body. Her purple sweater, blue jeans, and black Vans stood in deep contrast to the riding shoes and clothes that Ethan was wearing while he groomed the horse. She watched diligently as he cared for the horse, moving closer to him to listen to what he was whispering to Chocolate.

"You're a good horse," he whispered into Chocolate's ear, almost the same way Keenan spoke to Sonny. "I'm here to take care of you."

"Here, you try," he said to Lauren as he handed her the brush.

She finally grabbed it and lackadaisically brushed Chocolate.

While the horses were groomed, Xavier, another CJP alumnus, showed up at the ranch. Since he had started working his full-time job, weekends were the only time when he could help out. Like Jamie, he was pulled back to the ranch by the hope of returning something to the community and keeping the tradition of the ranch alive.

Xavier and Jamie walked the four young riders around the arena, as Mayisha had taught them years before. There was a system that, if performed correctly, would eventually replicate itself. It would be passed down from rider to rider, from generation to generation.

"Without them there is no program," Jamie said, looking at Ethan explaining to Lauren how to ride. "They are all that we have."

If finding a purpose for being there wasn't enough, Kenneth's next-door neighbor, Sylvester, was playing "Reasons" by Earth Wind & Fire loudly on his speaker system.

The song played loudly while they rode around the arena, barely avoiding the lumps of dirt that stood in the way. Jamie and Xavier had their reasons for being at the ranch and for wanting to ensure that it survived.

"We have to pick up the green stuff, too?" Ethan asked.

"Yes, you do," Jamie said while directing Lauren to grab the wheelbarrow and move it toward Chocolate's stall.

Since Anthony had broken his foot earlier in the week in a dirt-biking accident, Keenan and Tre had to work on the ranch more often. Keenan had since begun working again and was one of the managers at a local taco restaurant, while Tre continued to balance barber school with rodeo training.

"I'm just going to post up right here and watch y'all," Lauren said while the other three friends stepped inside Chocolate's stall to clean. "I got chased by the pony last week and it messed me up."

"You know if I ride the pony my feet will literally touch the ground," Isaiah said while scooping Chocolate's droppings with a shovel into the wheelbarrow.

"Penny is about to get mad at you," Star said to Lauren as she attempted to pet Penny.

"He looks so nice," Lauren said to Penny while petting

her nose. "How about you come help us clean these stalls?"

Everyone in the group laughed, making Tre take a break from cleaning Luke's stall to see what the commotion was about. He smiled when he realized what the kids were laughing about, remembering his first days on the ranch.

"OMG, he's pooping!" Star shouted.

"Last time I was here, I saw that horse pee and then you walked in it!" Lauren yelled to Isaiah.

"No, I didn't!" he fired back while Penny neighed loudly.

"Is she going to jump over the rail?" Lauren asked.

"No, silly, it's too high for her to jump over," Star replied. "If you try and pet her and lose a finger, don't blame it on me!"

"What's up, bro? Can I pet you?" Lauren asked Penny while standing on the other side of the metal gate.

Penny neighed furiously, making Lauren jump back.

"Oh no!" she said as she followed Isaiah and Lauren out of the stalls.

Ethan stayed back in Chocolate's stall, eagerly completing the task Jamie had told him to finish until he realized his friends had left.

"Hey, wait for me!" he said while running out of the stall.

Keenan continued to watch the youth riders from inside one of the stalls as they walked the horses around the arena. He saw the riders smile and laugh and live out a childhood that he wished he had experienced. *These are different types of kids*, he thought to himself. These were young people who were never forced to compromise their childhood.

After walking around the arena a few times, Lauren looked with deep confusion at the obstacle course that Jamie had set up while they were riding.

"So basically we're training like those horses?" she asked Jamie.

Everyone laughed at Lauren's question and began running around the obstacles the same way Chocolate or Sonny would have done.

"I ain't got time for all this!" Lauren said as she trailed behind. "I hope this helps your butt!"

Tre struggled to pull a trash can full of horse droppings across the arena, taking a break in the middle of the arena to catch his breath.

"God dang, this is heavy," he said while wiping the sweat off his forehead.

Keenan and Tre finished cleaning a couple of the horse stalls, joined the group, and began to help saddle and groom the horses. Keenan helped Lauren clean out Sonny's horseshoes with a hoof pick while Tre helped Star put a saddle on Helio.

"This horse moves a lot," Star said to Tre. She stood a few feet behind Tre while he tightened the rope on the metal gate.

"You just have to be calm yourself, if you want him to be

calm," Tre said in a tone that suggested he had handled hundreds of unruly horses throughout his lifetime. "It's going to be okay, don't be scared."

When both horses joined together in the middle of the arena, Tre and Keenan began speaking in Jamaican accents, which threw the children off.

"You don't see no rasta?" he asked the group in a voice he had been perfecting for years.

"Why you talking like that?" Lauren asked.

"Because me a raaaaasta, boy, Kingston, Jamaica," he said. "Why you no think meh a rasta boy?"

"Man, you're crazy!" Lauren yelled.

"Meh crazy. Meh crazy about these horses!" he replied, inciting laughs among everyone in the group.

Byron arrived just in time to hear what he thought sounded like people speaking with Jamaican accents in the arena. He wore a short-sleeved green T-shirt and blue jeans that nearly covered his burgundy Chuck Taylor shoes, and he was smoking a cigar.

"What's g-g-going on over there?" he said as Destiny, a six-year-old girl who had been sitting under the shaded canopy, looked on.

"Oh, hello," he said to Destiny.

"Hi," she replied.

Tre's championship belt shined in the sun while he leaned back from the crowd of people and began to bark directions in his normal voice. "So, the half circle is basically to space y'all out," he said, walking backward as the youth riders rode in a circle by themselves. "We have to maintain good spacing and keep all of the horses the same distance from one another. Everyone try to stay as close to the rails as possible, and the bigger the circle you make the longer the circle has to be."

The riders slowly pulled the reins on their horses and moved closer to the rails.

"Just keep kissing and kicking," Tre said, referring to the sounds they needed to make to keep the horses moving.

While the youth program had slowly begun to move forward in the past two weeks with the help of many of the cowboys and Compton Jr. Posse alumni, the ranch also continued to slowly deteriorate around them.

The *Compton Jr. Posse* sign that for so many years had pleasantly invited visitors into the ranch was slowly falling down. The bottom half of the words had fallen on the ground next to a pile of loose gravel. Like the community around it, the sign stood with resilience despite the challenges it faced.

On top of that, seeing the type of kids the youth program was attracting made Keenan think about who to target the program to.

"Our generation of riders were the backyard boogie kids," he said to Anthony while leaning on the metal ranch gate. "We didn't have it this good, which is why it's so funny to see this now. Me and my friends never did schoolwork when we came to the ranch, and we weren't as nice as these kids. We used to be back here cussing and fighting and messing with girls. And we need those type of kids here, too."

# ALRIGHT, THEN

**THOUGH MIMI LOVED HORSES,** she almost never joined Keiara at the ranch, preferring instead to stay in the comfort of her home. But today wasn't an ordinary day. It was the last time her granddaughter and great-granddaughter would be at the ranch for the foreseeable future.

Keiara had decided it was time to move back to Houston and was at the ranch to say goodbye to her horse, her friends, and the cowboys. It had always been her dream to return to Texas after moving back to Compton following her brother's death, but life, a near miscarriage, and the eventual birth of her daughter had altered her plans.

Her love for Houston began when she first learned about

Houston's black cowboys, some of whom competed in the Bill Pickett Rodeo in Los Angeles when she was seven. She remembers the way they rode around the arena with a style and swagger that she had never seen in Compton before. They spoke with drawl that felt familiar. Houston, she imagined, was a place where her black skin and her love for horses could exist without judgment.

"Houston is where I've always been able to grow and blossom," she said while leaning on her grandmother's shoulder and Al Green's "Love and Happiness" played on her cell phone on the table in front of her. "I always saw myself ending up there." Whenever she was in Houston, her mind felt free, so immersed was she in the black cowboy culture there. It was like no other place in the world. A place where nobody looked twice if they saw a black woman wearing a cowboy hat.

Nearby, a few of her close friends and their children had gathered and sat reminiscing about their time together. Like the black-inked tattoo of a cross that covered Keiara's arm and extended down into her hand, her move to Texas was inspired by faith in something that she could not yet see but believed deep in her soul.

Keiara wasn't as prepared to move to Houston as she would have liked to be. She didn't have a job lined up and would have to rely on her close friend Jazz, a fellow black barrel racer, to accommodate her and Taylor until she was able to find housing and earn money from competing in the circuit. On top of that, the memory of some of her past Houston experiences haunted Keiara: the nights that she was homeless and had to sleep in abandoned apartments without gas or electricity. These memories reminded her of how she learned to stretch a hundred-dollar bill for weeks while figuring out which friend to lean on next.

Still, despite her complicated past in the city, Keiara believed that Houston would be different this time around.

This time she had Penny and Taylor and was more committed than ever to becoming the first black woman at the National Finals Rodeo.

"This move is bringing me one step closer to my dream," she said to her grandmother as more of her friends and family began to arrive at the ranch. "God brought me back to Compton when my brother was killed and I didn't fight it, but now he's taking me back to Texas." She'd been waiting for this for the past five years.

While Keiara's excitement was palpable, people like her grandmother might suffer because Keiara was pursuing her dream. With Keiara gone, it would be difficult for Mimi to find someone to drive her to and from her medical appointments, which could potentially impact her health.

Randy joined the group, carrying a large box of fried chicken and potato wedges for everyone to share. The loss of Keiara would be felt throughout the ranch, and though their strong personalities often clashed, seeing her leave was like seeing one of his relatives go. That was why he offered to trailer her horse to Houston the next week.

While the group of friends hung out by the arena, Eugene and Tre practiced their roping on a wooden bull nearby as a trio of farriers worked on some of the horses' shoes in the garage. At this point of the year, the white farrier had been replaced by two high-school-aged Latinos and a black man.

Taylor played with her cousin Melrose in the arena. The two friends played around one of the dirt mounds, unaware that this would be one of their last times on the ranch together. They ran and galloped around the arena, emulating the horses that trotted nearby.

"Horsiieeeeee," Taylor yelled as Penny trotted away from her.

Taylor would be too young to remember what the ranch meant to her and the peace her mother felt when she brought her there. But even in a city like Houston, Keiara wanted her daughter never to forget about the city that they had both survived.

Keiara looked at Taylor while she galloped around the arena. Her milk-chocolate skin and her pigtails reminded her of herself when she was that age. While Compton's own black riding legacy ran in her blood, moving Taylor to a city where black cowboys and cowgirls were the norm and not the exception was, in her mind, worth the struggle. Together they were a team, and they'd grown used to adapting to new situations. Sometimes they didn't have a place to stay in Compton, so they knew a thing or two about struggle. Keiara felt this was almost like a form of training—that she'd put Taylor through a lot—but the reward was that they'd reach a permanent place of stability in Texas.

*At the end of the day*, she thought, *if your dream doesn't scare you, then it isn't a big enough dream.*

After saying goodbye to Keiara, Tre drove in the direction of the riding arena in Palos Verdes while Eugene sat in the passenger seat looking out at the world around him as they crossed Compton's borders. Dilapidated residential homes with potholed streets and graffitied walls were replaced by verdant eucalyptus trees, lush gardens, and well-maintained roads as they approached the opulent Palos Verdes community.

A typical membership at the Palos Verdes riding arena could cost upward of five thousand dollars for initiation and an eight-hundred-dollar monthly fee. But with the help of Big Al and Terry, two elder black riders who knew Tre's father, Tre, Eugene, and other local Compton riders got the chance to use the state-of-the-art facilities for calf roping practice throughout the week.

The practice session was divided into two sections, the first of which involved riding a horse and simulating roping the calf, the second running toward a roped calf, flipping it on its back, and quickly tying its legs up with a rope. Though Tre preferred bareback riding over calf roping, it was becoming one of his favorite events the more time he spent with Al and Terry.

"You ready to go?" Al asked Tre, who stood by the metal door waiting for the calf to shoot out of it on Al's remote-control command.

"Yep, let's do it," Tre responded.

Al pressed the button, and within seconds the calf was released into the arena. It ran full speed ahead while Tre sprinted toward it with reckless abandon and chased it down the same way he had successfully done in arenas around the country for the past few years. When he finally reached the calf, he slammed his knee into the calf's chest and flipped its body into the air, using the force of both of his arms before slamming it on its side and tying its legs with a rope.

"Whew!" Tre yelled, still panting from the rush of adrenaline that flowed through his body while the calf lay roped in front of him.

Al proudly looked at Tre as he got up from the ground and walked back in his direction.

"Not bad," he said to Tre. "You're pretty fast, but I bet I can beat you in the forty-yard dash."

Tre looked at Al with a smile. "Man, you're crazy," he said.

"Ok, maybe not the forty, but how about a ten-yard dash?" Al responded.

Terry, Eugene, and the rest of the guys laughed at Al's wishful thinking.

"Tre, you look a bit tired?" Terry said, still leaning on the gate as the sun set. "Boy, at your age you aren't supposed to be tired!"

The group of friends practiced until the sun completely set on the eucalyptus trees that surrounded the arena. It felt like paradise, because it was. It was cowboy paradise, for a group of cowboys from Compton.

Keiara walked around her apartment the next morning, still wearing a black headwrap around her hair from the previous night. In a day she and Taylor would be boarding a plane for Houston, far away from the only community her daughter had ever called home.

Taylor squirmed in her room, not yet fully awake, still tired from galloping with Melrose around the ranch the day before. It was the first day of April, but nothing about their move to Houston was a joke. In a day, Taylor's entire world would change, and she would be removed from her grandmother and great-grandmother and forced to adjust to an entirely new life.

Keiara's largest concern was to find a way to move her horse to Houston, but when Randy and Tre offered to drive

Penny there for her, things suddenly became easier for the twenty-nine-year-old single mother. Otherwise, it would have cost nine hundred dollars to rent a trailer.

Moving in with her friend Jazmine, whom she had known since she was a child, was another deciding factor for her move. The two friends had both dreamed about making the national finals since they were children, and with each other to rely on for support, their dreams finally seemed attainable.

"She's one of the few people that rides horses out there that I know," Keiara said. "But a lot of people out there believe in me, and I know I'm not going to have a stall when I get there, and my back is still injured, but I have faith in God that it'll all work out even though a lot of people here are doubting my decision to leave."

She didn't have a job lined up, but she had a dream, and for Keiara, that was more than enough.

"My journey in Compton is done, and to know that some riders in Houston believe in me is a blessing," she said. "I don't feel the same love here, and I know all that I've been going through is to help me make and become one of the first black women in the national rodeo finals."

Taylor hurried back down from the upstairs bedroom and into the living room to find her favorite Saturday morning film, *Frozen*, still on the big-screen television. It had now been a few days since she and Keiara had arrived in Cypress, a rural suburb filled with hundreds of housing developments forty minutes northeast of Houston, and both were slowly adjusting to the pace of their new lives.

At this point in her life, Taylor had grown accustomed to sleeping with the sounds of the police helicopters and sirens that echoed throughout Compton. The quiet and stillness of the Texas nights, in deep contrast, made her uneasy, and she found herself nervously reaching for Keiara's touch her first few nights in Cypress.

As Keiara and Taylor drove to Dairy Queen earlier that morning, the gravity of the move finally dawned on her as their car drove past vast fields of green pasture that, unlike the Richland Farms, seemed to stretch for miles without an end in sight. *Man*, she said to herself, *it's for real now*. She glanced at Taylor, who was on her iPad as R & B played out of the car speakers.

Watching *Frozen* every morning since she arrived was the closest thing to the schedule Taylor had back in Compton. She yelled at the screen like it was her first time seeing the movie. But living in a home with other people, including Jazmine's two adopted, similar-aged daughters, meant that it would no longer be just her and her mother. In addition, Jazmine's mother, a Compton-bred woman from Mimi's generation, lived nearby and enforced a strict napping and eating schedule every time she was at the house, filling part of the gap that Mimi had left since they last saw each other over a week ago.

With two stories, several bedrooms, a garage, and a backyard that led directly into a two-hundred-acre pasture with grazing cows, Jazmine's home was the largest that Keiara and Taylor had ever lived in. Having a home that size was something Keiara had wanted for Taylor, and though she knew she could stay with Jazmine only until she was able to get back on her feet, the idea of owning something similar was a dream of Keiara's.

With the money that she had saved and the rodeo purses she could earn at weekend barrel-racing events, it would be months before she would be able to afford to move out. And although Jazmine urged her to find a part-time job in the meantime, rodeo was the only thing that she had come to Texas to do. As a fellow Compton-native, Jazmine took it upon herself to do everything in her power to help Keiara and Taylor adjust. Though they weren't related by blood, the two considered each other sisters after having lived in each other's homes at different points in their lives.

Like Keiara, Jazmine had made the journey from Compton to Houston almost ten years earlier. She arrived on a bus with two duffle bags full of clothes, a saddle, and a hundred dollars in her pocket. It was the look in Keiara's eyes that Jazmine understood—a blend of desire and sacrifice, part of the code that she had learned riding horses on the farms.

Jazmine also worried that at some point reality would, like it did to her several times, kick her sister harder than a heavy-footed quarter horse. Rodeo was a gamble, and to succeed in it you had to spend money to make money. Sometimes competitors wouldn't bring home any purses. Sometimes they would leave having lost hundreds of dollars in fees down the drain. At some point, Keiara would have to learn about this on her own, especially after being denied government assistance by the state of Texas, but until then all Jazmine could do was support her sister's dream.

As one of the best women rodeo competitors in the state and one of its most respected, Jazmine also understood what it felt like to come from a city where rodeo wasn't as widely accepted as it was in Texas. Jazmine got tired of having to explain that people in California didn't only surf or ride surfboards; they competed in rodeo, too.

In California, the women's rodeo circuit was not as fully integrated into the Women's Professional Rodeo Association, a diverse organization that championed the experiences of women's rodeo, as it was in Texas. Most black women rodeo competitors in Houston were a part of it, which contributed to the camaraderie of the competitors. People wanted to see each other win amid tough competitions in ways that didn't happen in California. Maybe it was the idea that rodeo had a longer lineage in Texas, or maybe it was that in California rodeo competitors had fewer chances to compete and were fighting for scraps. In Texas, black rodeos were made for entire families to attend. They were as much about holding on to a piece of history as they were ensuring the future of black rodeo life, providing events like the leadline for children under the ages of seven to compete in.

Two of Jazmine's light brown saddles proudly sat on a chair, each with a *2016 Ladies Barrel Racing Champion* inscription on both sides. Taylor wasn't at the age when she could understand what the inscription on the saddles meant, or understand the blood, sweat, and tears that went into winning the rodeo championship that year. She was too young to know that Jazmine and her mother were part of one of the last generation of riders from Compton—too young to understand that her mother's desire to be a champion was the very reason she had decided to move her from their home.

Something about Jazmine's saddles drew Taylor to them. She played with them, tracing her tiny index finger around each letter, perhaps forecasting her own life as a future rodeo champion one day.

Though it was only her first week in Houston, Keiara immediately felt the support that Jazmine and other members of the black rodeo community had shown her. Living with her reminded her of the community of supporters that she had always dreamed of having: black women who rode horses and danced to Zydeco, a Louisiana-influenced dance, after big rodeo competitions. Living with Jazmine also reminded her of the secret handshake they had created as children, the same handshake that they promised to use to congratulate each other from the winner's podium at the national finals one day.

Keiara rubbed her hand across the tattoo of Mimi's name on her right arm and thought about what her grandmother was doing that morning while Taylor played with the saddles. Mimi was one of the people Keiara had told about her move, choosing not to tell her own mother because of their strained relationship. Living thousands of miles away from Mimi didn't stop Keiara from communicating a few times a day. Living in Cypress sometimes felt like a transplanted version of Compton, especially when Keiara cooked the same meatloaf and greens that Mimi had taught her how to make while episodes of *Martin* played loudly on the television, familiar Compton slang that only they knew rolling smoothly from both of their tongues.

Back in Compton, the cowboys were also leaning heavily on hope. The future of the ranch was uncertain, and because the ranch restoration project that Randy had designed never gained the traction he had hoped for, he realized that keeping the ranch alive in the meantime would require the same community effort that once made it succeed more than thirty years ago.

Every meeting with a potential sponsor or donor could have

been the answer to the ranch's financial woes. Not securing funding, however, didn't deter them from continuing to be the change that they wanted to see in the community. They organized canal cleanups, and Byron and his friends were determined to ensure the survival of the next generation of Compton's black cowboys by drawing more of Compton's youth to their Saturday morning classes. Even if every horse had to get sold, the cowboys weren't going to go down without a fight, despite being born into a world with their backs firmly against the wall.

The hardships that the ranch was experiencing were, ironically, doing more to bring the cowboys together than they did to keep them apart. When Myron, one of the original black riders from the farms, heard that its future was up for grabs, alongside other members of the community he helped the cowboys install panels for new stables.

Myron looked at the shirtless tattooed men who worked together to lift the heavy metal panels from one side of the ranch to the other. Drops of sweat poured from their bodies as they worked to improve their ranch the way cowboys on the farms and throughout the South had done for centuries. These were the same shirtless boys who used to stare at Myron and the other black elders in awe when they would dress up in neatly tailored, western-style clothing on Sundays, hoping to emulate them one day.

★ ★ ★

"Lord, please bless this rodeo and help us ensure that everyone who competes today walks away as healthy as they arrived and leave without injury. Lord, we ask you bless us on this holy day and continue to bless us," the rodeo announcer said into a microphone from a room high above the arena as the hot Texas weekend sun glared down on everyone. "Okay, it's time to rodeo!"

Though it would be months before Keiara's back injury allowed her to compete, the announcer's words brought her the biggest smile of the day. If she were back in Compton, Keiara would have been at home on a Sunday. But in Texas, every weekend brought a new rodeo, sometimes several in one day.

Taylor and Jazmine's daughter, Kade, watched closely while Jazmine and the other women prepared their horses and rode around the arena in front of their friends and family in the bleachers. The riders loosened the reins on each of their horses and made kissing sounds from their pursed lips while the horses' hooves made fresh tracks. Keiara watched and wished she was healthy enough to join the group in the arena, but she knew that everything worked in God's time. She also wished that her life hadn't brought as many challenges as it had over the past few years. Part of her wished that her brother was still alive to see her move closer to her dream. But another part of her knew that Gerrod—and other black men like Black, Marcus, Slim, and the ghosts of other fallen

Compton Cowboys—would be with her wherever she went.

The sounds of Zydeco played loudly on speakers that had moved the hips of black cowboys and cowgirls for decades. An elderly couple partner-danced near their pickup truck while holding on tightly to the brims of their beige Stetson hats, drawing cheers from onlookers. The smell of some of the county's best barbeque came out of someone's smoky grill and drifted into the sky. A familiar laugh from an unfamiliar face caused her to look in that direction. Everything in Keiara's life was perfect: the sounds, the smells—all felt like home because, in more ways than she could ever know, it all was home.